Pat Sloan and Jane Davidson

The Splendid Sampler

100 Spectacular Blocks from a Community of Quilters

Martingale®
Create with Confidence

The Splendid Sampler: 100 Spectacular Blocks from
a Community of Quilters
© 2017 by Pat Sloan and Jane Davidson

Martingale®
19021 120th Ave. NE, Ste. 102
Bothell, WA 98011-9511 USA
ShopMartingale.com

Printed in China
22 21 20 19 18   8 7 6 5 4 3

Library of Congress Cataloging-in-Publication Data
Names: Sloan, Pat (Patricia A.), author. | Davidson, Jane (Quilter),
    author.
Title: The splendid sampler : 100 spectacular blocks from a
    community of quilters / Pat Sloan and Jane Davidson.
Description: Bothell, WA : Martingale, 2017. | Includes index.
Identifiers: LCCN 2016047944 (print) | LCCN 2016048620 (ebook) |
    ISBN 9781604688092 | ISBN 9781604688108
Subjects: LCSH: Patchwork--Patterns. | Quilting--Patterns.
Classification: LCC TT835 .S554496 2017 (print) | LCC TT835 (ebook)
    | DDC 746.46--dc23
LC record available at https://lccn.loc.gov/2016047944

MISSION STATEMENT

We empower makers who use fabric and yarn
to make life more enjoyable.

CREDITS

**PUBLISHER AND
CHIEF VISIONARY OFFICER**
Jennifer Erbe Keltner

CONTENT DIRECTOR
Karen Costello Soltys

MANAGING EDITOR
Tina Cook

ACQUISITIONS EDITOR
Karen M. Burns

TECHNICAL EDITOR
Ellen Pahl

COPY EDITOR
Sheila Chapman Ryan

DESIGN MANAGER
Adrienne Smitke

PRODUCTION MANAGER
Regina Girard

COVER DESIGNER
Kathy Kotomaimoce

PHOTOGRAPHER
Brent Kane

ILLUSTRATOR
Anne Moscicki
Sandy Huffaker

CONTENTS

INTRODUCTION

We started The Splendid Sampler Sew-Along with a shared idea: to bring the whole world together to quilt. And with help from quilters across the globe, that's exactly what we did. More than 23,000 quilters—including many who'd never quilted before—joined our sew-along on Facebook and on our website, TheSplendidSampler.com.

One hundred quilt blocks, 83 designers, 12 months, and one goal: to experience the joys of a quilting life.

As the Splendids shared their blocks online week by week, we began to see the impact of our idea. Quilters shared their perfect points as well as their missed stitches; they celebrated breathtaking moments of beauty and offered encouragement when anyone experienced a setback. Inspiration, tips, techniques—and so many sewing stories!—filled the group's Facebook page. Block by block, we all learned new skills, met new challenges, and made new friends. That's the magic of quiltmaking.

Now that you have The Splendid Sampler at your fingertips—whether you've made all of the blocks, some of the blocks, or if you've never heard of The Splendid Sampler until now—you can walk the same magical path.

Up to now we've been talking about the blocks. But then there are the quilts! The finished quilts range from fun and colorful to chic and

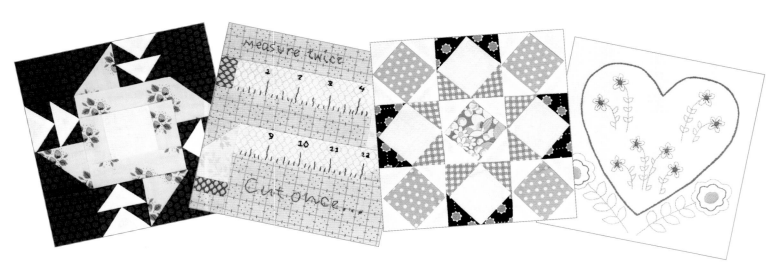

Many of The Splendid Sampler block designers. (Photo: Gregg Sloan)

sophisticated. And just plain pretty! But don't listen to us gush—flip to page 138 for a gallery of inspiring examples, visit ShopMartingale.com/SS17 for instructions on turning your beautiful blocks into quilts, and then head over to TheSplendidSampler.com for more ideas. When you're ready, you can add your Splendid Sampler quilt to the mix.

The Splendid Sampler has a long and happy life ahead. Gather your friends, host meet-ups, take time for a little stitching and friendship, and visit us online. Make splendid blocks together and enjoy the journey!

~ Pat & Jane ~

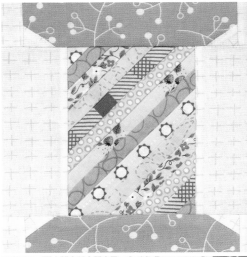

Visit TheSplendidSampler.com for links to the block designers' websites, plus bonus projects, technique tutorials, and much more.

For instructions on turning your blocks into finished quilts, visit ShopMartingale.com/SS17.

Wings

• JANE DAVIDSON •

Being part of a quilting group at my local shop was a wonderful way to cultivate new friendships and learn about the craft I loved. I always remember the first friendship quilt we made together: a sampler of charming butterfly blocks. Each block was as individual as the person who created it. ~Jane

What You'll Need

A: 26 assorted light print squares, 1½" × 1½"

B: 5 assorted light print squares, 2" × 2"

C: 5 assorted dark print squares, 2" × 2"

Embroidery floss: black

Assembly

Press all seam allowances in the directions indicated by the arrows.

1. Sew four A squares together to make a four-patch unit that is 2½" square. Press. Make four units.

Make 4.

2. To make the butterfly units, refer to "Triangle Squares" on page 135. Draw a diagonal line from corner to corner on the wrong side of the five B squares. Place each B square right sides together with a C square. Sew, cut, and press; trim the units to 1½" square. Make 10.

Make 10.

3. Sew two matching butterfly units and two A squares together in a four-patch arrangement to complete the butterfly; press. The unit should measure 2½" square. Make five.

Make 5.

4. Arrange the four-patch and butterfly units in three rows as shown, noting the direction of each butterfly. Join the units in rows and press. Join the rows to make a block that is 6½" square, including seam allowances.

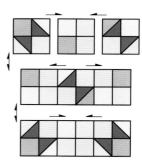

5. Trace the butterfly antennae stitching pattern onto the block for each butterfly, referring to the photograph. Using two strands of floss, backstitch the antennae.

Antenna

Lina's Gift

• PAT SLOAN •

I met Lina years ago when I first joined a quilting guild. One day, she was making darling little basket blocks with a group of quilters who were making a basket quilt as a gift for a friend. That opened my eyes to what it means to be a quilter. Lina's gift helped me appreciate quilters who put thousands of hours into a project and then give it with love to someone else. ~Pat

What You'll Need

Assorted tan prints:

   A: 3 squares, 2½" × 2½"

   B: 1 square, 4" × 4"

   C: 1 square, 2" × 2"

   D: 2 rectangles, 2" × 5"

Assorted brown prints:

   E: 3 squares, 2½" × 2½"

   F: 1 square, 4" × 4"

Assembly

Press all seam allowances in the directions indicated by the arrows.

1. Referring to "Triangle Squares" on page 135, use the A and E squares to make six half-square-triangle units (one is extra). Trim to 2" square.

Make 6.

2. Repeat step 1 with the B and F squares. Trim to 3½" square. Make two units; one is extra.

Make 2.

3. Arrange four half-square-triangle units from step 1, one unit from step 2, and the C square in two rows. Sew the smaller units together and press. Sew them to the larger unit and press. The unit should measure 5" square.

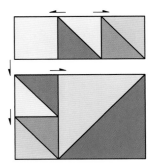

4. Sew the remaining half-square-triangle unit from step 1 to a D rectangle and press. Sew the D rectangles to the unit from step 3 as shown.

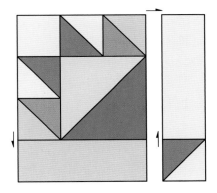

Lots of Love

• MELISSA CORRY •

Whether it's a special gift for a marriage, a welcome for a new baby, an expression of sympathy at the passing of a loved one, or just cuddly warmth, quilts wrap the special people in our lives in lots of love. This block represents the six people in my life whom I always want to wrap in love— my husband and five amazing children.
~Melissa

What You'll Need

5 dark print squares, 5" × 5";
   cut *each* square into:
   A: 2 rectangles, 1½" × 2½"
1 dark print square, 5" × 5"; cut
   into
   B: 2 rectangles, 2½" × 4½"
1 fat eighth of light print; cut into:
   C: 2 squares, 2½" × 2½"
   D: 14 squares, 1½" × 1½"
   E: 20 squares, 1" × 1"

Assembly

Press all seam allowances in the directions indicated by the arrows.

1. Referring to "Stitch and Flip" on page 136, draw a diagonal line from corner to corner on the wrong side of the 20 E squares. Place a marked square on an A rectangle, right sides together. Stitch, trim, and press. Repeat on the opposite corner as shown. Make 10 units, two of each color.

Make 2 of each
color, 10 total.

2. Draw a diagonal line from corner to corner on the wrong side of five D squares. Place a marked square on a step 1 unit with right sides together, as shown. Stitch, trim, and press as before. Make five units, one of each color.

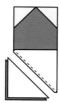

Make 1 of each
color, 5 total.

3. Repeat step 2 to sew marked D squares to the remaining step 1 units, but place the diagonal line in the opposite direction as shown. Make five units, one of each color.

Make 1 of each
color, 5 total.

4. Pin and sew together two same-color units to make a small heart. Press. The heart should measure 2½" square. Make five small hearts.

Make 5.

5. Repeat steps 1–4 using the B, C, and remaining D pieces to make one large heart. Sew the D squares to the top of the rectangles and sew a C square to the bottom of each. The large heart should measure 4½" square.

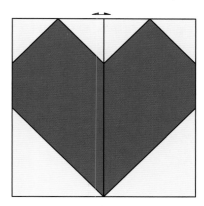

Make 1.

6. Lay out the five small hearts and the large heart as shown. Sew two small hearts together, one above the other, taking care to match seam intersections. Press. Join to the side of the large heart and press. Sew the remaining three small hearts together side by side, matching seams, and then sew to the bottom of the large heart unit. Press.

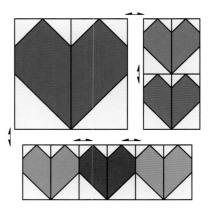

ALTERNATE COLORWAY

Melissa made her hearts scrappy and tied them all together with a unifying background fabric. Why not let the special people in your life each choose a fabric for their heart? Or use their favorite colors for a special keepsake block.

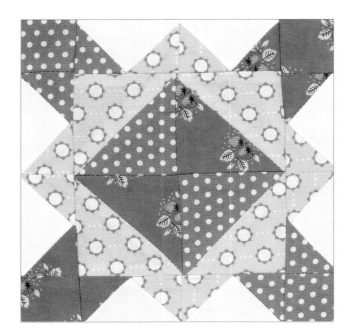

Focal Point

• NATALIA BONNER •

I named my block to commemorate a defining moment in my sewing journey. After quitting my "real" job and buying a long-arm quilting machine, I sat down with my sister and she helped me figure out who I am and where I needed to focus my attention, leading to a happy career in the quilting industry. In this block, I see arrows pointing toward the center, the focal point. ~Natalia

What You'll Need

1 piece, 4" × 10" *each,* of yellow, red, and green prints, cut into:

A: 2 yellow squares, 3" × 3"

B: 8 yellow squares, 1½" × 1½"

C: 1 red square, 3" × 3"

D: 6 red squares, 1½" × 1½"

E: 1 green square, 3" × 3"

F: 6 green squares, 1½" × 1½"

G: 8 white solid rectangles, 1½" × 2½"

Assembly

Press all seam allowances in the directions indicated by the arrows.

1. Draw a diagonal line from corner to corner on the wrong side of all of the A and B squares and four of the D and F squares.

2. Place an A square right sides together with the C square. Referring to "Triangle Squares" on page 135, sew, cut, and press to make two half-square-triangle units. Trim the units to 2½" square. Repeat with the remaining A square and the E square, pressing in the opposite direction.

Make 2 of each.

3. Arrange and sew the four units together as shown. Press. The unit should measure 4½" square.

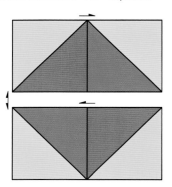

4. Place a marked D square on the bottom left corner of a G rectangle. Referring to "Stitch and Flip" on page 136, sew, trim, and press. Place a marked B square on the bottom right corner of the unit and repeat to make a flying-geese unit. Make two units. The units should measure 1½" × 2½".

Make 2.

5. Repeat step 4 to make two units but reverse the fabric placement.

Make 2.

6. Repeat steps 4 and 5 with B and F squares on a G rectangle. Make two of each unit.

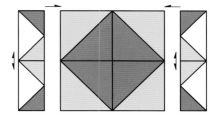

Make 2 of each.

7. Arrange and sew four of the flying-geese units and the center unit from step 3 together as shown. Press. The unit should measure 6½" × 4½".

8. Arrange and sew two D squares, two F squares, the remaining flying-geese units, and the unit from step 7 as shown to complete the block.

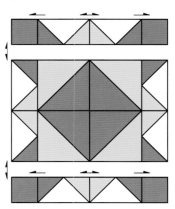

ALTERNATE COLORWAY

Whether you choose dark, light, or bright fabrics, keep in mind that the pieces are rather small, so sticking to small-scale prints works well.

Checkerboard

• PAT SLOAN •

For a very long time I've had a vision of the ultimate one-patch quilt. Teeny, tiny squares, only 1" each. Can you imagine row upon row of lovely little scraps put into a quilt? I've been cutting my scraps into 1½" squares for, yes, a quilt of tiny squares. My checkerboard block is a mini version of this. It would be an amazing full-sized quilt, don't you think? ~Pat

What You'll Need

A: 3 blue print strips, 1½" × 11"
B: 3 navy print strips, 1½" × 11"

STARCH FIRST

When making these small blocks, I experimented with starching my fabric before cutting. I found that a nice firm fabric resulted in a more accurate block. Spray starch the fabric before you cut; let it dry, and then press. Now it's ready for you to cut strips for the checkerboard block.

~Pat

Assembly

Press all seam allowances in the directions indicated by the arrows.

1. Sew an A strip to a B strip to make a strip set. Press. Make three strip sets. Cut each strip into six segments, 1½" wide, for a total of 18.

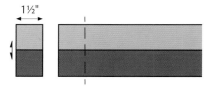

Make 3 strip sets. Cut 18 segments.

2. Sew two segments together as shown to make a four-patch unit. The unit should measure 2½" square. Make nine.

Make 9.

3. Sew the four-patch units together in groups of three to make a row and press. Sew the rows together to make the block.

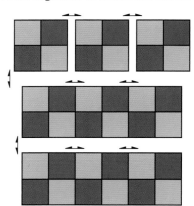

Simple Simon

· CELINE PERKINS ·

Quilting gives me joy. I love the process, the discovery, the community, and the finished product. I also love figuring out an easier or faster way to do things. With this block, it happened by accident when I considered strip piecing the corner units. I realized that I could simply make a nine-patch unit first. My family teases me because of this constant effort to make things easier. ~Celine

What You'll Need

A: 5 red print squares, 2½" × 2½"

B: 4 black print squares, 2½" × 2½"

C: 2 gold print rectangles, 1" × 3¼"

D: 1 gold print rectangle, 1" × 6½"

Assembly

Press all seam allowances in the directions indicated by the arrows.

1. Arrange and sew the A and B squares into a nine-patch unit as shown and press. It should measure 6½" square.

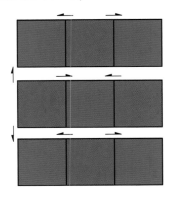

2. Cut the nine-patch unit into quarters that measure 3¼" × 3¼".

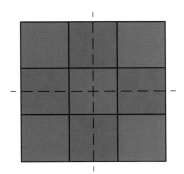

3. Sew the C rectangles between the block quarters as shown and press. Sew the D rectangle between the units and press.

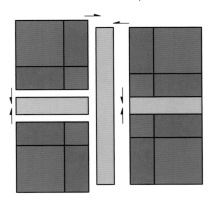

Scrap Star

• COREY YODER •

If you're a scrappy rock star, then this is the block for you! I've long said that the best bits of fabric can be found at the bottom of your scrap bin. They're the little bits of fabric too dear to part with and yet too small to be worked into many projects. This block is just perfect for those yummy, scrappy pieces you've been saving. ~Corey

What You'll Need

4 assorted print charm squares*, 5" × 5"; cut *each* into:

A: 1 square, 1⅞" × 1⅞"; cut in half diagonally to yield 2 triangles (1 is extra)

B: 1 square, 1½" × 1½"

1 white solid square, 10" × 10"; cut into:

C: 2 squares, 1⅞" × 1⅞"; cut in half diagonally to yield 4 triangles

D: 4 squares, 1½" × 1½"

E: 2 rectangles, 1" × 4½"

F: 2 rectangles, 1" × 5½"

The block shown uses 8 different prints in the star points. To use different prints for the star points, cut the 1⅞" A squares from one print and the 1½" B squares from a second print of the same color.

1 green polka-dot square, 10" × 10"; cut into:

G: 4 rectangles, 1½" × 2½"

H: 4 squares, 1½" × 1½"

1 red print square, 10" × 10"; cut into:

I: 2 rectangles, 1" × 5½"

J: 2 rectangles, 1" × 6½"

K: 4 squares, 2½" × 2½"

Assembly

Press all seam allowances in the directions indicated by the arrows.

1. Sew each A triangle to a C triangle to make four half-square-triangle units. Press. The units should measure 1½" square.

Make 1 of each.

2. Sew the units together as shown to make a pinwheel unit that measures 2½" square. Press.

3. Referring to "Stitch and Flip" on page 136, make flying-geese units by sewing a B square to the left side of each G rectangle. Trim and press. Sew a D square to the right side to complete the flying-geese unit. Make one of each fabric combination.

Make 1 of each.

4. Arrange the flying-geese units and H squares around the pinwheel unit as shown so that like fabrics are next to each other. Sew together in rows and press. Join the rows. Press. The unit should measure 4½" square.

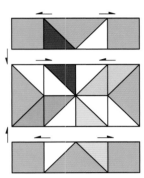

5. Sew an E rectangle to each side of the unit and press. Then sew F rectangles to the top and bottom. Press.

6. Sew an I rectangle to each side of the unit and press. Sew J rectangles to the top and bottom. Press.

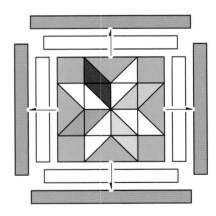

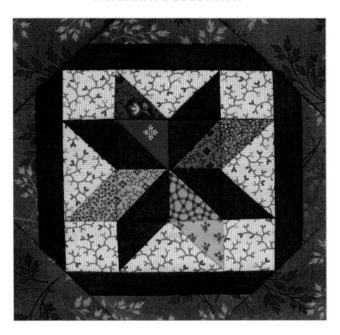

Placement of lights and darks seems to make another star appear in this version. The darks look as though they form a Friendship Star with a pinwheel of light diamonds swirling atop it.

7. Using the stitch and flip method, sew a K square to each corner. Trim and press.

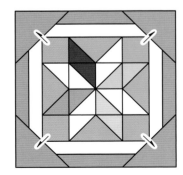

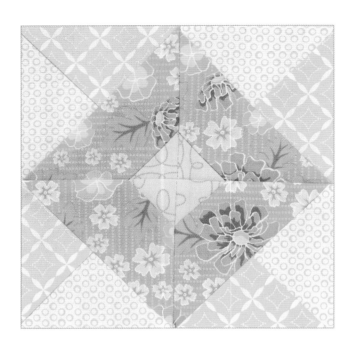

Pieces of Friendship

• LINDSAY MAYLAND •

At American Patchwork and Quilting, where I work, our contributors and editors may come from different places and enjoy different quilting techniques, but what ties us all together is the joy and community that quilting brings us. This block represents quilters coming together to share a passion and friendship. ~Lindsay

What You'll Need

A: 1 dark yellow print square, 4¼" × 4¼"; cut into quarters diagonally to make 4 triangles

B: 1 light yellow print square, 4¼" × 4¼"; cut into quarters diagonally to make 4 triangles

C: 2 peach print squares, 3⅞" × 3⅞"; cut in half diagonally to make 4 triangles

D: 4 light blue print squares, 1½" × 1½"

Assembly

Press all seam allowances in the directions indicated by the arrows.

1. Sew together an A and a B triangle as shown and press. Make four units.

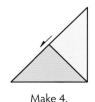

Make 4.

2. Add a C triangle to make a unit that measures 3½" square. Make four.

Make 4.

3. Referring to "Stitch and Flip" on page 136, draw a diagonal line on the wrong side of each D square. Align a marked square with the C corner of a square unit as shown. Sew, trim, and press. Repeat with each square unit.

4. Arrange and sew the four square units together in rows of two and press. Join the rows to make the block. Press.

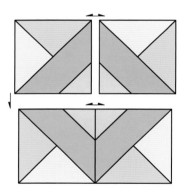

Family Stars

• KIMBERLY JOLLY •

My block represents all the little stars in my life. My four children (Emma, William, Peyton, and Christopher) are the four stars and anchors of my world. The red star in the center is me, the pink star is Emma, and the three blue stars are my boys. They are the reason I do most everything, whether it's running my business or indulging my passion of quilting. ~Kimberly

What You'll Need

4 assorted print pieces,
4½" × 7½"; cut *each* into:

A: 6 squares, 1¼" × 1¼"

B: 1 square, 2" × 2"

1 light print fat eighth; cut into:

C: 12 rectangles, 1¼" × 2"

D: 5 squares, 2" × 2"

E: 4 squares, 1¼" × 1¼"

F: 8 red print squares, 1¼" × 1¼"

Assembly

Press all seam allowances in the directions indicated by the arrows.

1. Referring to "Stitch and Flip" on page 136, draw a diagonal line from corner to corner on the wrong side of the A and F squares.

2. Place a marked A square on one corner of a C rectangle. Sew, trim, and press. Repeat on the opposite corner with a matching A square to make a flying-geese unit. Make two of each color for a total of eight.

Make 2 of each.

3. Use the same method to sew A and F squares to the corners of four D squares, noting the fabric placement for each unit. Sew, trim, and press; make four units as shown.

Make 1 of each.

4. Arrange the flying-geese units, the units from step 3, four B squares, four C rectangles, and the remaining D square into rows as shown. Sew the units into rows and press. Join the rows and press.

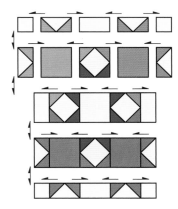

Iowa

• SHERRI MCCONNELL •

My maternal grandmother taught me to quilt, and she absolutely loved the Snowball block and often used it in her quilts and projects. I designed a scrappy Snowball block because my grandmother also held a great appreciation for scraps—she found ways to save, store, and use even the smallest bits of quilting fabric. ~Sherri

What You'll Need

A: 8 light print squares, 2" × 2"

B: 1 red print rectangle, 2" × 6½"

C: 2 gold print rectangles, 2" × 3½"

D: 2 navy print rectangles, 2" × 3½"

E: 1 brown print rectangle, 2" × 6½"

Assembly

Press all seam allowances in the directions indicated by the arrows.

1. Draw a diagonal line from corner to corner on the wrong side of each A square.

2. Referring to "Stitch and Flip" on page 136, align an A square on each corner of the B rectangle as shown, noting the direction of the diagonal lines. Sew, trim, and press. Repeat with two A squares and the E rectangle.

Make 1 of each.

3. Use the Stitch and Flip method to sew an A square to each of the C and D rectangles as shown, noting the direction of the drawn lines and pressing arrows.

Make 1 of each.

4. Sew the matching rectangle units from step 3 together into rows as shown. Press. Join the four units together and press.

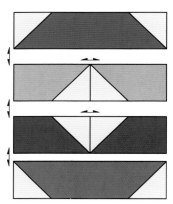

Sweet Candy

• KRIS THURGOOD •

The center of this block reminds me of a piece of scrumptious wrapped candy. I own a quilt shop, and customers often comment that it must be like working at a candy store. How true! Every day I have the opportunity to share something sweet with those who walk through the doors. The love of sewing is a sweet thing indeed—and it has zero calories! ~Kris

What You'll Need

A: 1 tan print square, 3" × 3"

B: 2 tan print squares, 2½" × 2½"

C: 1 red print square, 3" × 3"

D: 1 red print square, 2½" × 2½"

E: 4 teal print squares, 2½" × 2½"

Assembly

Press all seam allowances in the directions indicated by the arrows.

1. Referring to "Triangle Squares" on page 135, draw a diagonal line from corner to corner on the wrong side of the A square. Place it right sides together with the C square. Sew, cut, and press to make two half-square-triangle units. Trim to 2½" square.

Make 2.

2. Arrange the two half-square-triangle units, B squares, D square, and E squares in rows as shown. Sew into rows and press. Join the rows and press.

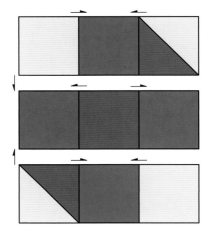

MAKE IT SWEETER

Experiment with color placement or fussy cutting. The center square and two triangles look like a candy wrapper. Contrast those pieces with the surrounding squares, and the candy shape pops! Use stripes, word fabrics, or a motif that fills the center square. Our Internet group created amazing variations.

~Pat

Hand in Hand

• KARI CARR •

With an abundance of patience and kindness, my mom shared her knowledge of sewing and crafting with me when I was very young. She had dainty hands that made beautiful things for our home. I loved to watch her create. In this block, the red center represents her heart. Radiating from her to future generations, we will go hand in hand, creating, sewing, and loving. ~Kari

What You'll Need

A: 2 light print squares, 3½" × 3½"

B: 8 light print rectangles, 1¼" × 2¾"

C: 2 teal print squares, 3½" × 3½

D: 4 red print squares, 1½" × 1½"

E: 1 red print square, 2" × 2"

F: 4 gold print F shapes using the pattern on page 21

Assembly

Press all seam allowances in the directions indicated by the arrows.

1. Draw a diagonal line from corner to corner on the wrong side of the A and D squares.

2. Referring to "Triangle Squares" on page 135, place an A square on a C square with right sides together. Sew, cut, and press to make two half-square-triangle units. Trim the units to 2¾" square. Make four.

Make 4.

3. Referring to "Stitch and Flip" on page 136, place a D square on the C corner of a half-square-triangle unit. Sew, trim, and press. Make four.

Make 4.

4. Fold an F piece in half lengthwise, wrong sides together. Place the folded F piece on the right side of a B rectangle, aligning the edges as shown. Place a second B rectangle on top, right sides together. Sew through all layers using a ¼" seam allowance. Make four units.

Fold.

Make 4.

5. From the right side, open the F piece and refold and flatten it so that the center is aligned with the seamline. Press to create a triangle. Repeat for each unit. The units should measure 2" × 2¾".

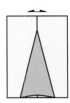

6. Arrange and sew the pieced units and the E square in rows as shown. Press. Sew the rows together and press.

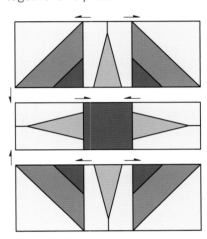

ALTERNATE COLORWAY

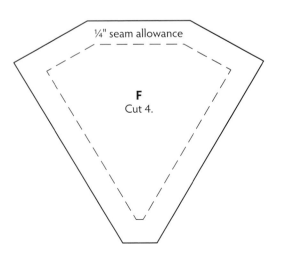

Changing the fabric palette to three lights and a dark shifts the focus to the Churn Dash emerging from the center of the block. The sunny yellow fabric pairs well with the ray-like shapes.

¼" seam allowance

F
Cut 4.

Inspector Sidekick

• MICHELE FOSTER •

I began sewing and quilting about a year after my first cat, Pal, came to live with me. When the quilting bug hit me, Pal did whatever he could to help: stealing thread spools, lying in the middle of freshly washed fabric, and chewing through serger thread. Never a dull moment with a furry sidekick around! ~Michele

What You'll Need

A: 4 red print squares, 1½" × 1½"

B: 4 light print squares, 1½" × 1½"

C: 4 light print rectangles, 1½" × 2½"

D: 8 blue print squares, 2" × 2"

E: 4 gold print squares, 2" × 2"

F: 4 pink print squares, 2" × 2"

G: 1 brown print square, 2½" × 2½"

Assembly

Press all seam allowances in the directions indicated by the arrows.

1. Sew the A and B squares together in pairs and press. The units should measure 1½" × 2½".

Make 4.

2. Sew a C rectangle to each unit from step 1 to make two of each as shown. Press. The corner units should measure 2½" square.

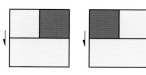

Make 2 of each.

3. Referring to "Triangle Squares" on page 135, draw a diagonal line from corner to corner on the wrong side of the eight D squares. Layer the squares right sides together with the E and F squares. Sew, cut, and press to make eight half-square-triangle units of each color combination. Trim the units to 1½" square.

Make 8.   Make 8.

4. Arrange and sew two matching half-square-triangle units together as shown. Press.

Join the pairs to make units that measure 2½" square. Make four.

Make 4.

5. Arrange the pieced units and the G square in three rows as shown, noting the orientation of the corner units. Sew the units into rows and press. Join the rows and press.

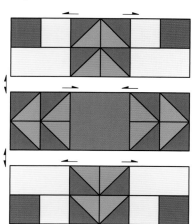

Simple Surprises

· AMY ELLIS ·

I'm a big fan of quilts and blocks that look more complicated than they actually are. Cutting beautiful pieces of fabric and sewing them together into a simple block is always rewarding. Sewing blocks together into a quilt to create movement and depth is even more rewarding! ~Amy

What You'll Need

A: 1 green print square, 4" × 4"

B: 1 red print square, 4" × 4"

C: 2 navy print squares, 2½" × 2½"

D: 2 red check rectangles, 1½" × 2½"

E: 2 red check rectangles, 1½" × 3½"

Assembly

Press all seam allowances in the directions indicated by the arrows.

1. Referring to "Triangle Squares" on page 135, draw a diagonal line from corner to corner on the wrong side of the A square. Place the square right sides together with the B square. Sew, cut, and press to make two half-square-triangle units. Trim the units to 3½" square.

Make 2.

2. Sew a C square to the right edge of each D rectangle and press. Sew an E rectangle to the top. Press. The unit should measure 3½" square. Make two units.

Make 2.

3. Arrange and sew the units together in two rows as shown. Press. Join the rows and press.

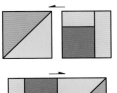

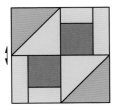

Lemonade

• AMY GIBSON •

When life turns sour, quilters can be the sweetener. After discovering that I had to rip out all of the quilting from a fairly large quilt, I fretted and cried. Then I hosted an "un-quilting party" that filled my house with friends and infused the quilt with sweet memories. This block honors the quilting friends who helped me make lemonade from lemons. ~Amy

What You'll Need

A: 6 assorted light print squares, 2½" × 2½"

B: 4 assorted green print squares, 2½" × 2½"

C: 2 different red print squares, 2½" × 2½"

D: 4 assorted yellow print squares, 2" × 2"

E: 2 different light print squares, 2" × 2"

Template plastic

Assembly

Press all seam allowances in the directions indicated by the arrows.

1. Referring to "Triangle Squares" on page 135, draw a diagonal line from corner to corner on the wrong side of the six A squares.

2. Place a marked A square right sides together with each B square. Sew, cut, and press to make eight half-square-triangle units. Trim each unit to 2" square.

Make 8.

3. Repeat step 2 with the remaining A squares and the C squares to make four half-square-triangle units.

Make 4.

4. Make plastic templates using the concave and convex pattern pieces on page 25. Trace the template and cut a convex quarter circle from two of the D squares.

Trace and cut concave corner pieces from the two E squares.

5. Place a concave piece right sides together on a convex piece (the curves will be facing in opposite directions). Pin the center point, and then pin the two ends. Ease in the remaining edges and pin. Sew slowly using a ¼" seam allowance and removing pins as you sew. Press. The unit should measure 2" square. Make two units.

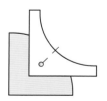

Make 2.

6. Arrange the half-square-triangle units, the curved units, and the remaining two D squares in four rows as shown. Sew the units into rows and press. Sew the rows together and press.

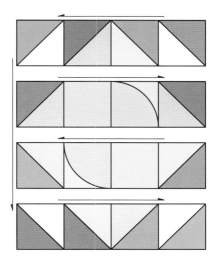

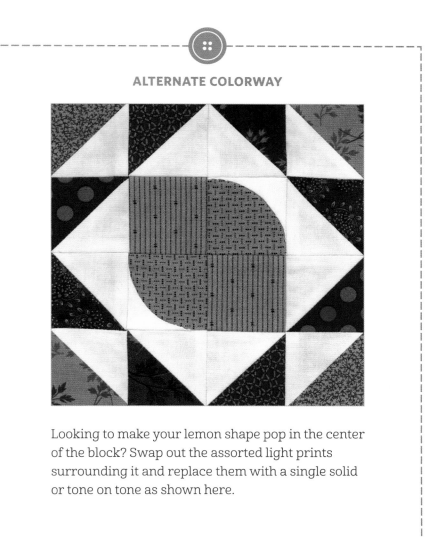

ALTERNATE COLORWAY

Looking to make your lemon shape pop in the center of the block? Swap out the assorted light prints surrounding it and replace them with a single solid or tone on tone as shown here.

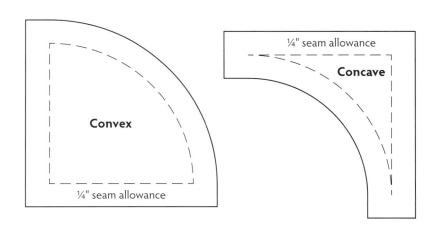

Convex

¼" seam allowance

¼" seam allowance

Concave

Dashing by Chocolate

• LAURA FLYNN •

I learned to knit and sew by the time I was in sixth grade. When I found quiltmaking, I quickly became addicted to cutting up fabric and sewing it back together! The Churn Dash block has always been a favorite—I added flying geese here for interest. As for chocolate, well, everything is better with chocolate! ~Laura

What You'll Need

A: 2 cream print squares, 3" × 3"

B: 4 cream print rectangles, 1½" × 2½"

C: 2 red print squares, 3" × 3"

D: 8 light red print squares, 1½" × 1½"

E: 4 salmon print rectangles, 1½" × 2½"

F: 1 brown print square, 2½" × 2½"

Assembly

Press all seam allowances in the directions indicated by the arrows.

1. Draw a diagonal line from corner to corner on the wrong side of the A and D squares.

2. Referring to "Triangle Squares" on page 135, layer a marked A square right sides together with a C square. Sew, cut, and press to make half-square-triangle units. Make four units and trim to 2½" square.

Make 4.

3. Referring to "Stitch and Flip" on page 136, place a marked D square on one end of an E rectangle, right sides together. Sew, trim, and press. Repeat on the opposite corner and press to make a flying-geese unit that measures 1½" × 2½". Make four.

Make 4.

4. Sew a flying geese unit to a B rectangle as shown. Press. The unit should measure 2½" square. Make four.

Make 4.

5. Arrange the units and the F square into three rows as shown. Sew into rows and press. Join the rows and press.

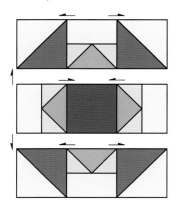

Friends around the Square

• JULIE KARASEK •

I named my block "Friends around the Square" because it reminds me of the first mystery quilt I made at a retreat. While I may do more visiting than sewing at a retreat, I love spending time with my quilting friends. ~Julie

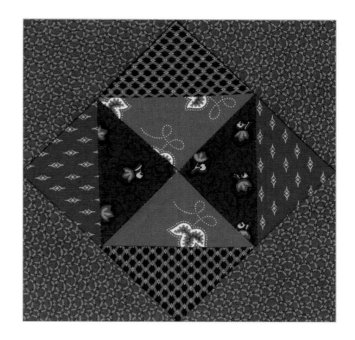

What You'll Need

A: 2 different red print squares, 3¼" × 3¼"

B: 2 different brown print squares, 3¼" × 3¼"

C: 2 matching navy squares, 3⅞" × 3⅞"; cut in half diagonally to make 4 triangles

Assembly

1. Place the A and B squares right sides together. Draw a diagonal line from corner to corner on the wrong side of the top square. Sew ¼" from each side of the drawn line. Cut on line and press the seam allowances open. Make four half-square-triangle units and trim to 2⅝" square.

Make 2 of each.

2. Sew the four units together as shown to make the block center and press.

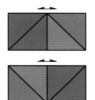 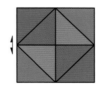

3. Sew C triangles to opposite sides of the block center. The corners of the triangle will extend beyond the center unit by ¼" on each side. Press. Repeat for the remaining sides and press.

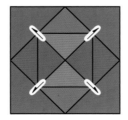

BE ADVENTUROUS

Don't be afraid to try new techniques. After all, it's only fabric! The worst thing that will happen is you may need to make another block. Make friends with your tools and keep a sharp seam ripper at your side to make any unsewing as quick and painless as possible.

~Julie

Swirltime

• SARAH J. MAXWELL •

Swirltime captures my love for pinwheel designs. Part of the appeal is how they remind me of my youth. Many warm summer evenings were spent in the back yard running with a "spinner" to see the colors change as the blades whirled. My block incorporates many different fabrics since I am definitely a "why use one fabric when you can use ten?" type of girl. ~Sarah

What You'll Need

2 light print pieces, 5" × 7"; cut *each* into:

    A: 2 squares, 2" × 2"

    B: 2 rectangles, 2" × 3½"

C: 4 assorted red print rectangles, 2" × 3½"

D: 4 assorted brown print squares, 2" × 2"

E: 2 navy print #1 squares, 2" × 2"

F: 2 navy print #2 squares, 2" × 2"

Assembly

Press all seam allowances in the directions indicated by the arrows.

1. Draw a diagonal line from corner to corner on the wrong side of each A, D, E, and F square.

2. Referring to "Stitch and Flip" on page 136, place a marked A square on the left end of a C rectangle as shown, noting the direction of the diagonal line. Sew, trim, and press. Make four units.

Make 4.

3. Repeat step 2, placing a D square on a B rectangle, again noting the angle of the diagonal line. Make four units.

Make 4.

4. Place an E square on the opposite end of the unit from step 3. Sew, trim, and press as before. Make two units with E squares and two units with F squares.

Make 4.

5. Sew a step 4 unit to a step 2 unit as shown and press. The unit should measure 3½" square. Make four units.

Make 4.

6. Arrange and sew the four units together as shown. Press.

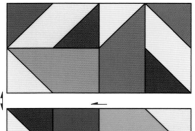

Flights of Friendship

• BARBARA GROVES & MARY JACOBSON •

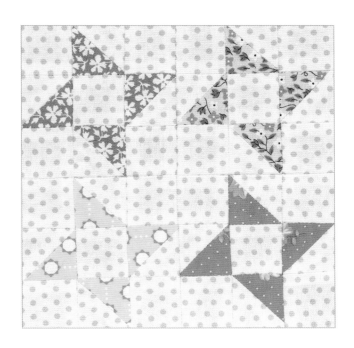

Less than a year after taking our first quilting class, we opened a quilt shop. That led to designing patterns and fabric. We've made so many friends along the way—we must be the luckiest girls in the world! Our block has four friendship stars, each representing a different aspect of our quilting journey.

What You'll Need

1 light print fat eighth; cut into:

    A: 8 squares, 2" × 2"

    B: 20 squares, 1½" × 1½"

4 assorted bright print squares, 5" × 5"; cut *each* square into:

    C: 2 squares, 2" × 2"

Assembly

Press all seam allowances in the directions indicated by the arrows.

1. Draw a diagonal line from corner to corner on the wrong side of the eight A squares.

2. Referring to "Triangle Squares" on page 135, place a marked square right sides together with each C square. Sew, cut, and press to make four half-square-triangle units of each bright print for a total of 16. Trim the units to 1½" square.

Make 4 of each print.

3. Arrange four matching units from step 2 with five B squares in three rows as shown. Sew the units together in rows and press. Sew the rows together. Press. The unit should measure 3½" square. Repeat to make a total of four units, one of each print.

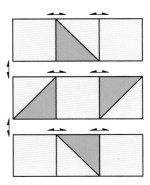

Make 1 of each print.

4. Arrange the four units into two rows of two and sew together as shown. Press.

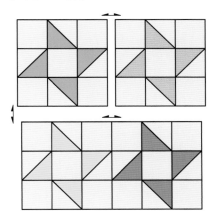

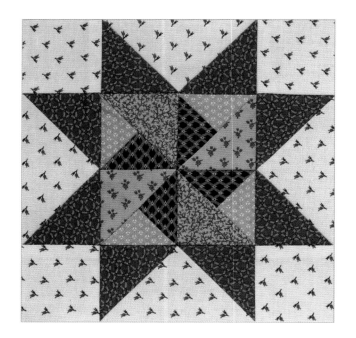

Whirling in Circles

• DEBBIE ROBERTS •

A lifelong quilter, I had always dreamed of someday owning a quilt shop, and 15 years ago my dream became a reality. Running a successful retail business—as well as designing, stitching, and writing patterns—keeps me whirling in circles. But I love what I do and wouldn't have it any other way. ~Debbie

What You'll Need

A: 1 gold print square, 2¾" × 2¾"; cut into quarters diagonally to yield 4 triangles

B: 1 brown print square, 2¾" × 2¾"; cut into quarters diagonally to yield 4 triangles

C: 1 pink print square, 2⅜" × 2⅜"; cut in half diagonally to yield 2 triangles

D: 1 pink print square, 2⅜" × 2⅜"; cut in half diagonally to yield 2 triangles

1 beige print piece, 5" × 9"; cut into:

    E: 1 square, 4¼" × 4¼"

    F: 4 squares, 2" × 2"

G: 4 blue print squares, 2⅜" × 2⅜"

Assembly

Press all seam allowances in the directions indicated by the arrows.

1. Join the A and B triangles as shown and press. Make four units.

Make 4.

2. Sew an AB unit to a C triangle. Press. Make two. Sew an AB unit to a D triangle. Make two. The units should measure 2" square.

Make 2 of each.

3. Join the units from step 2 to make the block center. Press. It should measure 3½" square.

4. Referring to "Fast Flying Geese" on page 135, make four flying-geese units with the E and G squares. The units should measure 2" × 3½".

Make 4.

5. Arrange the flying-geese units and the F squares around the block center and sew together in rows. Press. Join the rows and press.

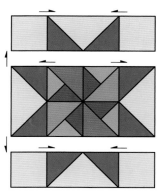

Rising Star

· KATHY BROWN ·

I learned to quilt by watching every episode of Simply Quilts *(my mother recorded them onto VHS tapes for me) and by reading a plethora of quilt books and magazines from cover to cover. With each new block I made, my piecing skills grew and my blocks became like "rising stars"—each one brighter and better than the last! ~Kathy*

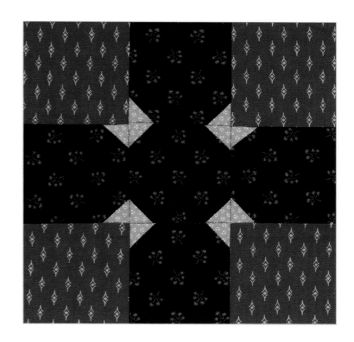

What You'll Need

A: 12 gold print squares, 1" × 1"
B: 5 navy print squares, 2½" × 2½"
C: 4 red print squares, 2½" × 2½"

Assembly

Press all seam allowances in the directions indicated by the arrows.

1. Draw a diagonal line from corner to corner on the wrong side of each A square.

2. Pin and sew marked A squares on two adjacent corners of a B square, referring to "Stitch and Flip" on page 136. Press. Make four units.

Make 4.

3. Repeat step 2 to sew a marked A square on each corner of the remaining B square. Press.

Make 1.

4. Arrange the pieced units and the four C squares in three rows. Sew together in rows and press. Join the rows and press.

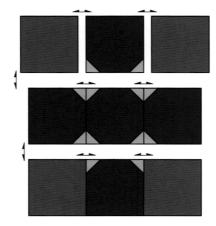

Minnesota Maze

· ROSEANN KERMES ·

My family, the Waldochs, has been growing vegetables and selling them at farmers' markets and at Grandpa Waldoch's roadside stand for over 100 years. My cousins now run the farm and each year plant a corn maze. My Minnesota Maze block looks like arrows pointing in all directions—just like a maze! It's fun to see the design develop as the pieces are sewn together. ~Roseann

What You'll Need

1 brown print piece, 8" × 10"; cut into:

  A: 1 square, 2½" × 2½"

  B: 4 rectangles, 1½" × 2½"

  C: 4 squares, 1⅞" × 1⅞"; cut in half diagonally to make 8 triangles

1 light print piece, 5" × 10"; cut into:

  D: 4 squares, 1½" × 1½"

  E: 4 rectangles, 1½" × 2½"

  F: 2 squares, 2⅞" × 2⅞"; cut in half diagonally to make 4 triangles

G: 12 pink print squares, 1½" × 1½"

Assembly

Press all seam allowances in the directions indicated by the arrows.

1. Draw a diagonal line from corner to corner on the wrong side of the D squares. Referring to "Stitch and Flip" on page 136, sew the D squares to the A square.

2. Draw a diagonal line from corner on the wrong side of eight G squares. Use the stitch-and-flip technique to sew them to the B rectangles to make four flying-geese units. Press. The units should measure 2½" × 1½".

3. Sew an E rectangle to a flying-geese unit. Press. Make four units that measure 2½" square.

Make 4.

4. Sew two C triangles to a G square. Press. Sew an F triangle to the unit and press. Make four units.

Make 4.

5. Arrange the units into three rows as shown. Sew into rows and press. Join the rows and press.

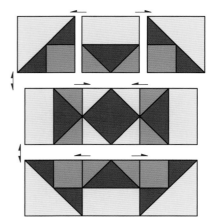

Hen and Chicks

• HEIDI KAISAND •

When I opened Hen & Chicks Studio, my happiness exploded. Running a retail store and a fully-equipped retreat center lets me offer inspiration and help people make quilts. It has been a joyful experience to encourage quilters and watch their creativity blossom. It also allows me time to be a mother hen to my own chicks, Henry, Goldie, and Virginia. ~Heidi

What You'll Need

A: 2 blue print squares, 2⅛" × 2⅛"; cut in half diagonally to make 4 triangles

B: 6 gold print squares, 2⅛" × 2⅛"; cut in half diagonally to make 12 triangles

C: 4 brown print squares, 3⅜" × 3⅜"; cut in half diagonally to make 8 triangles (4 are extra)*

D: 1 red print square, 1½" × 1½"

E: 4 cream print rectangles, 1½" × 3"

The block shown uses 4 different brown prints. Cut just 2 different brown print squares to yield 4 triangles for a less scrappy version.

Assembly

Press all seam allowances in the directions indicated by the arrows.

1. Sew an A triangle to a B triangle to make a half-square-triangle unit. Press. Make four units that measure 1¾" square.

Make 4.

2. Sew a B triangle to each remaining edge of the A triangle as shown. Press. Make four pieced triangle units.

Make 4.

3. Sew a C triangle to the long edge of the pieced triangle units to make a corner unit. Press. The unit should measure 3" square. Make four corner units.

Make 4.

4. Arrange the four corner units, the D square, and the E rectangles in three rows as shown. Sew the units into rows and press. Join the rows and press.

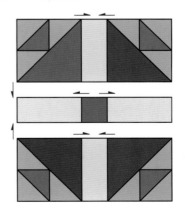

Traveler

• PAT SLOAN •

An unexpected and fun part of being a quilt designer is being invited to teach at shops and guilds. My husband and I drive to most of my events, which has allowed us to see so much of the United States. My Traveler block brings to mind an intersection or crossroads—and all the places where quilters live. What a great adventure it is to be a quilter! ~Pat

What You'll Need

A: 4 polka-dot squares, 2" × 2"

B: 4 floral print rectangles, 2" × 3½"

C: 4 white print squares, 2" × 2"

D: 4 orange print squares, 2" × 2"

Assembly

Press all seam allowances in the directions indicated by the arrows.

1. Draw a line from corner to corner on the wrong side of the A squares.

2. Place an A square on one end of a B rectangle and sew on the line, referring to "Stitch and Flip" on page 136. Make four units as shown and press.

Make 2 of each.

3. Sew a C and a D square together and press. Make four. Sew these units to the units from step 2 as shown and press. Make four units that measure 3½" square.

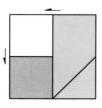

Make 4.

4. Arrange the units as shown so that the seam allowances will nest together. Sew into rows and press. Join the rows and press to complete the block.

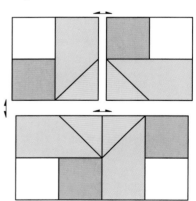

+ Love

- JENNIFER ALBAUGH -

I named this block + Love (Plus Love) for my family's business, Quiltique. Quiltique is a quilt shop run by me, my sister Kara, and our parents, Bob and Jan. We've been blessed to have grown a successful shop that's been in business for over 13 years. Each of us is represented in the four corners of the plus sign, but what binds us together is the center: love. ~Jennifer

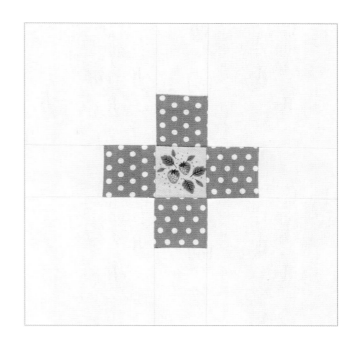

What You Need

A: 4 red polka-dot squares, 1½" × 1½"

1 white solid piece, 6" × 13"; cut into:

B: 4 rectangles, 1½" × 2"

C: 4 squares, 3" × 3"

D: 1 blue print square, 1½" × 1½"

Assembly

Press all seam allowances in the directions indicated by the arrows.

1. Sew an A square to each B rectangle and press to make four units that measure 1½" × 3".

Make 4.

2. Sew a C square to each side of a unit from step 1 and press. Make two units that measure 6½" × 3".

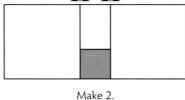

Make 2.

3. Sew the D square between the two remaining units from step 1. Press. The unit should measure 6½" × 1½".

4. Arrange the units as shown and sew together to complete the block. Press.

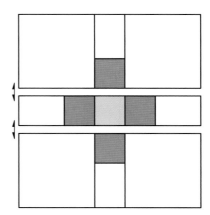

Happy Thoughts

• VANESSA GOERTZEN •

Every time I begin a new quilt, I find myself immersed in a happy place. I imagine all the adventures the quilt will experience: the laughter, the blanket forts, the picnics, and even the sick days full of snuggles. Quilting is truly a labor of love that fills me up with the happiest of thoughts. ~Vanessa

What You'll Need

1 navy print piece, 6" × 10"; cut into:

    A: 16 squares, 1¼" × 1¼"

    B: 2 squares, 2½" × 2½"

    C: 4 squares, 2" × 2"

1 white tone-on-tone piece, 5" × 8"; cut into:

    D: 8 rectangles, 1¼" × 2"

    E: 1 square, 2" × 2"

1 light blue print piece, 6" × 8"; cut into:

    F: 2 squares, 2½" × 2½"

    G: 2 rectangles, 1¼" × 2"

    H: 2 rectangles, 1¼" × 3½"

Assembly

Press all seam allowances in the directions indicated by the arrows.

1. Draw a diagonal line from corner to corner on the wrong side of the 16 A squares. Referring to "Stitch and Flip" on page 136, sew two marked A squares to each D rectangle to make eight flying-geese units. Sew the units together in pairs and press to make four units that measure 2" square.

Make 4.

SEWING ON THE LINE

To sew along a marked diagonal line using Stitch and Flip, sew next to the line, not on top. Sew on the side closest to the edge you'll trim to ¼". This allows for bulk in the seam allowance. When pressed, everything keeps a perfect rectangle shape.

            ~Vanessa

2. Draw a diagonal line from corner to corner on the wrong side of the two F squares. Referring to "Triangle Squares" on page 135, layer each marked F square with a B square. Make four half-square-triangle units and trim them to 2" square.

Make 4.

3. Sew a flying-geese unit to each half-square-triangle unit as shown. Press. Make four. The units should measure 3½" × 2".

Make 4.

4. Arrange and sew the E square together with the G and H rectangles to make the block center as shown. Press. The unit should measure 3½" square.

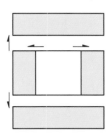

5. Arrange the block center, the units from step 3, and the four C squares as shown. Sew the units into rows and press. Join the rows; press.

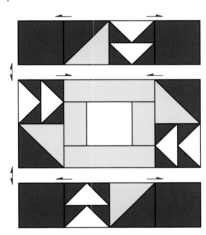

ALTERNATE COLORWAY

In blocks with numerous seams and lots of movement, such as this one, small nondirectional prints are a great choice. When sewn together, they offer a smoother transition from piece to piece.

Full Circle

· HOLLY DEGROOT ·

This block is a reminder of the first quilt I made, when I learned my sister-in-law was expecting. I appliquéd colorful circles onto white squares, and then joined them to make the quilt. For this design, I pieced together smaller bits to make a whole circle, because quilting, making things, and being creative make me feel whole, happy, and fulfilled. ~Holly

What You'll Need

A: 5 aqua stripe strips, 1⅛" × 4"

1 white solid piece, 7" × 15";
    cut into:
    B: 4 strips, 1⅛" × 4"

1 gray dot piece, 4" × 14"

Template plastic

Assembly

Press all seam allowances in the directions indicated by the arrows.

1. Lay out the A and B strips, alternating them and starting and ending with A strips. Sew the strips together along the long edges and press.

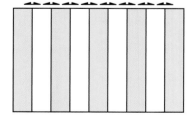

2. Make templates for the half circle and the background by tracing the patterns on page 39 onto the template plastic and cutting on the traced lines.

3. Place the half-circle template over the pieced rectangle from step 1, making sure the template is centered on the middle strip. Trace around the template and cut on the traced line to make the half circle. Mark the center and seam intersection alignment dots using a water-soluble marker. Stay stitch ⅛" from the edges all around the piece to stabilize the curved edges and ensure the seams don't come unsewn.

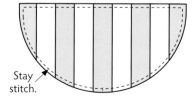

Stay stitch.

4. Cut a second half circle from the remainder of the white solid fabric and mark the center and seam intersections.

5. Trace the background template onto the gray dot fabric two times and cut out the pieces on the traced line. Mark the centers and seam intersections.

6. Place a half circle right sides together with a background piece, pinning carefully along the curve to match the centers, alignment dots, and the edges of the pieces. Snip about ⅛" into the seam allowance of the background piece to help with alignment. Sew carefully around the curve using a ¼" seam allowance and sewing with the half circle on the bottom. Sew slowly to ensure that the fabric doesn't bunch up along the curve. Press. Repeat with the second half circle and background piece. The units should measure 3½" × 6½".

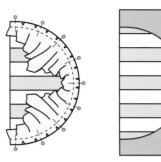

7. Join the units, matching seam intersections, and press.

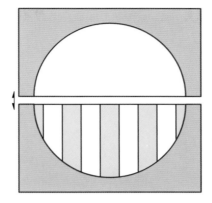

TO USE OR NOT TO USE

Don't hesitate to cut into your favorite bundle of fabric. It might look pretty sitting in a stack on your shelf, but you'll love it even more when it's sewn into a quilt you can cuddle up with on the couch!

~Holly

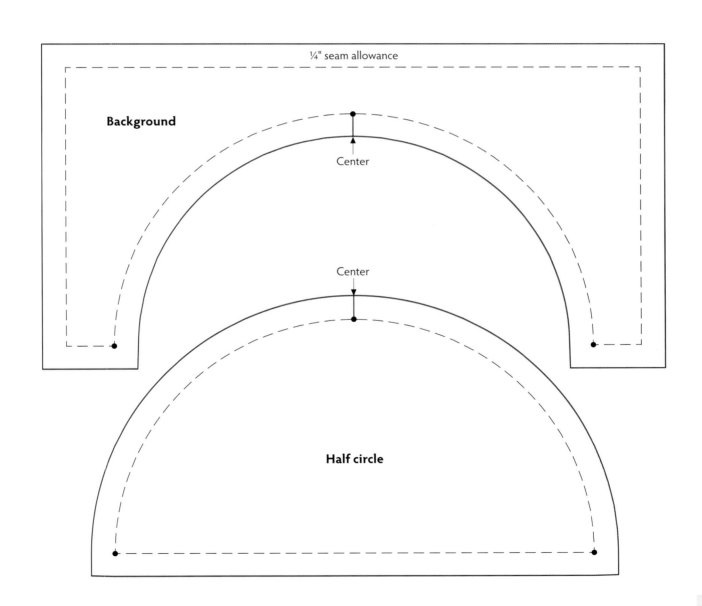

¼" seam allowance

Background

Center

Center

Half circle

Button Basket

• KAREN COSTELLO SOLTYS •

Antique baskets, handwoven baskets, pressed-cardboard berry-picking baskets (especially the turquoise ones)—I love 'em all. I treasure an antique market basket with 1"-wide oak slats that was handed down from my grandmother. And my hand sewing lives in a basket on my coffee table so it's always at the ready. If there's a basket quilt block to be had, sign me up! ~Karen

What You'll Need

1 cream print rectangle, 7" × 14"; cut into:

    A: 2 squares, 1½" × 1½"

    B: 2 squares, 1" × 1"

    C: 2 rectangles, 1½" × 3"

    D: 1 rectangle, 1½" × 6½"

    E: 1 rectangle, 6½" × 3"

F: 1 green print rectangle, 4½" × 2½"

1 brown stripe rectangle, 6" × 12"; cut into:

    G: 1 rectangle, 1" × 4½"

    H: 4 squares, 2½" × 2½"

    I: 1 bias strip, 1" × 8"

J: 4 teal polka-dot squares, 1⅞" × 1⅞"

2 small buttons for basket handles (⅜" to ½" diameter)

3"-diameter drinking glass

Assembly

Press all seam allowances in the directions indicated by the arrows.

1. Referring to "Stitch and Flip" on page 136, sew A squares on the two bottom corners of the F rectangle.

2. In the same manner, sew the B squares to the ends of the G rectangle. Sew this strip to the top of the F rectangle as shown, to make the basket rim. Press. The unit should measure 4½" × 3".

3. Sew the C rectangles to the basket sides, the D rectangle to the bottom, and the E rectangle to the top. Press. The unit should be 6½" square.

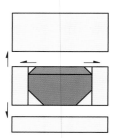

4. Press the I bias strip in half lengthwise, wrong sides together, to make the basket handle. Using the glass for a template, trace a curve onto the background fabric above the basket. Curve the bias strip just below the marked line with the raw edges matching the marked line; leave at least ½" of the strip ends below the top of the basket. Don't pull the handle too tight; you'll need lots of ease to flip over the handle after stitching. Stitch about ⅛" from the raw edges, starting and stopping at the edge of the basket and leaving the handle ends unsewn. Sew slowly and pivot often to achieve a smooth curve.

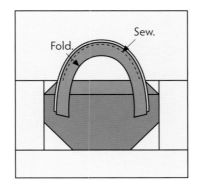

5. Flip the stitched bias strip up over the stitching and press flat. Machine or hand stitch the folded edge of the bias strip in place. Trim the raw ends at an angle but don't sew them down or turn them under.

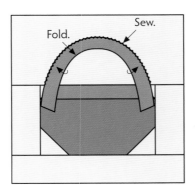

6. Place an H square right sides together on each corner of the block, with the stripe running horizontally. Using the stitch-and-flip technique as before, mark a diagonal line, sew, and press. Trim the excess H fabric from between the layers, but leave the background fabric intact. Repeat to sew a J square to each corner, trimming the excess J fabric only. Press well and stay stitch ⅛" from the outer edges.

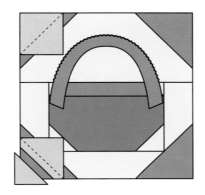

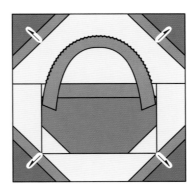

7. Sew a button on each side of the basket handle to secure the raw ends and give the look of a swing-handle basket.

BASKET-HANDLE OPTIONS

I learned to make this appliquéd bias-strip handle from noted quiltmaker Mimi Dietrich. It's quicker to sew than to explain! For an even faster option, adhere fusible web to a ¾"-wide bias strip, curve it along the marked line, and fuse in place. Or substitute rickrack for a whimsical look.

~Karen

Full-Circle Star

• VICTORIA FINDLAY WOLFE •

I can never resist using a polka-dot fabric in my quilts. I wear dots; I sew with them. I even eat them in the form of Dots candy! Adding a few polka dots to my quilts always freshens up the look. And adding a whole bunch *of appliquéd polka dots to a quilt really brings out the "Wow!" factor. ~Victoria*

What You'll Need

1 cream print piece, 7" × 13"; cut into:

    A: 5 cream print squares, 2½" × 2½"

1 gold print piece, 4" × 14"

1 navy print piece, 4" × 4", for appliqué

1 red print piece, 3" × 3", for appliqué

Template plastic

Freezer paper (optional)

Assembly

Press all seam allowances in the directions indicated by the arrows.

1. Make templates for the star points and background triangle using template plastic and the patterns on sheet 1. Cut four star points and four star points reversed from the gold print; cut four background pieces from the cream print.

2. Make templates for the circle and the arc using template plastic or freezer paper and the patterns. Prepare the circle appliqués from red print and the arcs from brown print using your favorite hand- or machine-appliqué method. Refer to "Needle-Turn Appliqué" on page 133 as needed.

3. Pin the red circles onto each A square and stitch by hand or machine. Appliqué the arc piece to one square to make the block center.

Make 4.

Make 1.

4. Sew a gold star point to each long side of a background triangle to make a star-point unit. Press.

Make four star-point units that measure 2½" square.

Make 4.

5. Arrange the A squares and star-point units in rows as shown. Sew the squares into rows and press. Join the rows, pinning at intersections of seams for accuracy, and press.

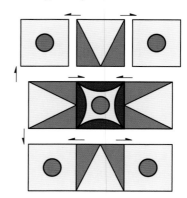

Circle of Friendship

· MICHELE MUSKA ·

When Darlene Zimmerman showed me how to use a Dresden template at my first quilt show, I immediately bought fabric and a sewing machine. The resulting Dresden Plate became a lily pad in my first art quilt, which still hangs in my studio. It reminds me daily that quilters form a special circle of friends. ~Michele

What You'll Need

A: 6 assorted print strips, 1½" × 6½"*

B: 16 assorted print rectangles, 2" × 2½"

Template plastic

Or use random-width strips.

Assembly

Press all seam allowances in the directions indicated by the arrows.

1. Join the A strips as shown to make a 6½" square. Press.

2. Make a plastic template using the Dresden wedge pattern at right. Trace the template onto each of the 16 B rectangles and cut a wedge from each.

3. Sew the wedge pieces together to make an arc. Press the seams in one direction.

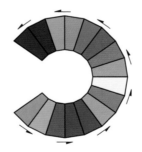

4. Position the arc on the background as shown. Pin in place and trim the excess fabric.

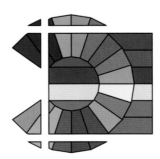

5. Fold the outer and inner raw edges of the arc under ¼" along the untrimmed edges and pin in place. Appliqué the arc to the background by hand or machine. **Note:** For quilting, Michelle used the quilt-as-you-go technique. To do that, layer and baste the block with batting and backing. Michelle stitched a large running stitch using 12-weight cotton thread.

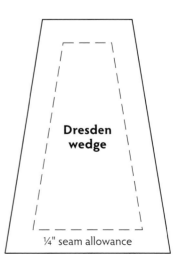

Dresden wedge

¼" seam allowance

Jersey

• CARRIE NELSON •

For a seemingly reserved woman, my Mom had an amazing fearlessness and independence. She said it was because she was a "Jersey girl," but I think it's because she knew she could face any challenge head-on. Through it all, she was always kind and smiling. Her favorite quilts usually had stars and always included something I'd added or changed. ~Carrie

What You'll Need

1 navy print piece, 5" × 10"; cut into:

    A: 1 square, 2½" × 2½"

    B: 8 squares, 1½" × 1½"

1 blue print piece, 4" × 8"; cut into:

    C: 2 rectangles, 1" × 2½"

    D: 2 rectangles, 1" × 3½"

1 cream print piece, 5" × 10"; cut into:

    E: 1 square, 4¼" × 4¼"

    F: 4 squares, 2" × 2"

G: 4 red print squares, 2⅜" × 2⅜"

Assembly

Press all seam allowances in the directions indicated by the arrows.

1. Sew C rectangles to opposite sides of the A square. Press. Sew D rectangles to the top and bottom of the unit. Press. The unit should measure 3½" square.

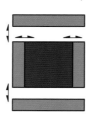

2. Referring to "Stitch and Flip" on page 136, sew a B square on each corner of the unit and press.

3. Referring to "Fast Flying Geese" on page 135, make four flying-geese units with the E and G squares. The units should measure 2" × 3½".

Make 4.

4. Using the stitch-and-flip technique as before, sew a B square to corner of each F square to make four corner units.

Make 4.

5. Sew the units into rows and press. Join the rows and press to complete the block.

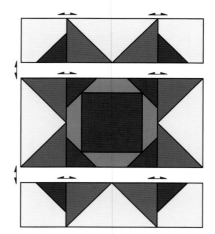

Prism

• SARA LAWSON •

I designed my block in honor of all of the friends I've met through sewing. As an introvert, I have trouble connecting with people. Sewing has given me a reason to meet many friends, both online and in person, from all over the world. I find that I have no difficulty talking with people about sewing and it's really helped me blossom and become a better and more empathetic person. ~Sara

What You'll Need

A: 1 light print rectangle,
 3½" × 3¼"

B: 1 light blue plaid rectangle,
 2¼" × 3½"

C: 1 stripe rectangle, 1¼" × 5"

D: 1 gray print strip, 1" × 3½"

E: 1 navy print rectangle, 1" × 1¼"

F: 1 navy print strip, 1½" × 4¼"

G: 1 navy tone-on-tone rectangle,
 1¼" × 2"

H: 1 light blue print strip, 1¼" × 5"

I: 1 light blue floral strip, 2" × 6½"

Assembly

Press all seam allowances in the directions indicated by the arrows.

1. Sew A to B and press. Sew C to the right side and press to make unit 1, which should measure 4¼" × 5".

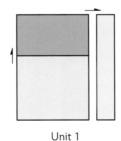

Unit 1

2. Sew D to E and press. Sew F to the top and press to make unit 2. The unit should measure 4¼" × 2".

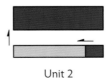

Unit 2

3. Sew G to H and press to make unit 3. The unit should measure 1¼" × 6½".

Unit 3

4. Join unit 1 to unit 2 and press. Sew unit 3 to the right side, and then add piece I to the left side to complete the block. Press.

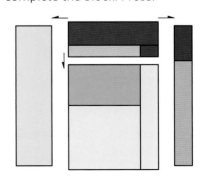

Unity Star

• VANESSA CHRISTENSON •

I center all my choices in life around my family, taking into consideration how they will improve, affect, and mold our family unity and health. I created the center star to represent our family unit and all the pieces around it are different choices, protecting and keeping it together. ~Vanessa

What You'll Need

A: 1 red print square, 2½" × 2½"

B: 20 white tone-on-tone squares, 1½" × 1½"

C: 4 white tone-on-tone squares, 2½" × 2½"

D: 8 red check squares, 1½" × 1½"

E: 8 navy print squares, 1½" × 1½"

F: 4 green polka-dot squares, 2½" × 2½"

Assembly

Press all seam allowances in the directions indicated by the arrows.

1. Draw a diagonal line from corner to corner on the wrong side of each B, D, and E square.

2. Referring to "Stitch and Flip" on page 136, sew four small squares on each larger A, C, and F square, making the units as indicated. Each unit should measure 2½" square.

3. Arrange the nine units in rows as shown to create the star in the center. Sew the units into rows and press. Join the rows and press to complete the block.

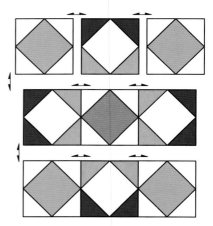

Make 1.

Make 4.

Make 4.

Make 4.

Sunshine

• KIM NIEDZWIECKI •

This simple block was inspired by a sweet pencil pouch I made for my daughter Katy. Every year I sew a new pouch for her to make her smile when she sees it. She is my little bit of sunshine, so it's a sunshine block! ~Kim

What You'll Need

A: 4 assorted yellow print squares, 1½" × 1½"

B: 8 assorted navy print squares, 1½" × 1½"

C: 8 assorted light blue print squares, 1½" × 1½"

D: 4 red polka-dot rectangles, 1½" × 2½"

E: 4 red check rectangles, 1½" × 2½"

Assembly

Press all seam allowances in the directions indicated by the arrows.

1. Sew the four A squares together to make a four-patch unit. Press. It should measure 2½" square.

2. Sew two B squares and two C squares together to make a four-patch unit that measures 2½" square. Press. Make four.

Make 4.

3. Sew a D rectangle to an E rectangle and press. Make four units that measure 2½" square.

Make 4.

4. Arrange the units in three rows. Sew the units into rows and press. Join the rows and press to complete the block.

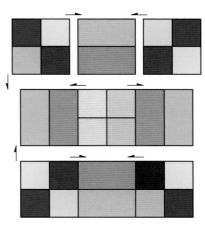

From Colorado to the Midwest

• EBONY LOVE •

One of my early commissions as a quilter was to create a reproduction of an 1877 quilt. It included the Colorado block, which I loved since I grew up there. I've lived in four states since, eventually settling in the Midwest. I've reimagined the Colorado block to represent my journey. ~Ebony

What You'll Need

1 white solid piece, 6" × 10";
  cut into:
  A: 2 squares, 2⅜" × 2⅜"; cut in
    half diagonally to make"
    4 triangles
  B: 1 square, 4¼" × 4¼"; cut
    into quarters diagonally to
    make 4 triangles

1 green print piece, 4" × 10";
  cut into:
  C: 2 squares, 2⅜" × 2⅜"; cut in
    half diagonally to make
    4 triangles (1 is extra)
  D: 1 square, 1¼" × 1¼"
  E: 1 rectangle, 1¼" × 2"

1 blue print piece, 4" × 10";
  cut into:
  F: 2 squares, 2⅜" × 2⅜"; cut in
    half diagonally to make 4
    triangles (1 is extra)
  G: 1 square, 1¼" × 1¼"
  H: 1 rectangle, 1¼" × 2"

1 red print piece, 4" × 10"; cut into:
  I: 2 squares, 2⅜" × 2⅜"; cut in
    half diagonally to make 4
    triangles (1 is extra)
  J: 1 square, 1¼" × 1¼"
  K: 1 rectangle, 1¼" × 2"

1 aqua print piece, 4" × 10";
  cut into:
  L: 2 squares, 2⅜" × 2⅜"; cut in
    half diagonally to make 4
    triangles (1 is extra)
  M: 1 square, 1¼" × 1¼"
  N: 1 rectangle, 1¼" × 2"
  O: 4 yellow print squares,
    1¼" × 1¼"

Assembly

Press all seam allowances in the directions indicated by the arrows.

1. Sew an A triangle to a C triangle to make a half-square-triangle unit. Press. Repeat to sew A triangles to F, I, and L triangles to make one unit of each color. The units should measure 2" square.

Make 1 of each.

2. Sew a C triangle and an F triangle to a B triangle as shown to make a flying-geese unit. Press. Repeat with the remaining B triangles, adding C, F, I, and L triangles as shown to make one unit of each color combination. The units should measure 2" × 3½".

Make 1 of each.

3. Sew the D square to an O square and press. Sew the E rectangle to the side and press. Repeat to make one unit of each color as shown. The units should measure 2" square.

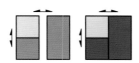

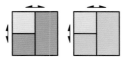

Make 1 of each.

4. Sew the units from step 3 into a four-patch unit for the block center and press. The block center should measure 3½" square.

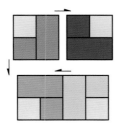

5. Arrange the half-square-triangle units, the flying-geese units, and the block center in three rows as shown. Join the units into rows and press. Sew

the rows together and press to complete the block.

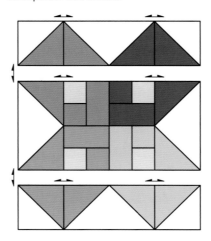

ALTERNATE COLORWAY

Pay attention to the pressing arrows on this block's seams. Though it might not be your norm, pressing seam allowances open will help reduce the bulk where multiple seam allowances intersect.

PRESSING AID

My go-to tool for pressing seams open is a pressing stick, The Strip Stick, along with a hot, dry iron. The tool elevates the seam above the block, allowing you to isolate it while the seam is supported. Moisture can distort fabric, so I don't use steam or starch while piecing blocks.

~Ebony

A Girl's First Purse

• DI MILL •

The very first thing I remember sewing as a young girl was a purse. I was so proud of it. I carried it to church and on shopping trips to the city. It was slightly different in structure than this block, but I loved that purse and thought I was very stylish whenever I walked around with it in my hand. ~Di

What You'll Need

A: 12 assorted print squares, 1½" × 1½"

1 cream print piece, 5" × 15"; cut into:

    B: 4 squares, 1½" × 1½"

    C: 2 rectangles, 1½" × 3½"

    D: 2 rectangles, 2" × 6½"

2 small buttons

Assembly

Press all seam allowances in the directions indicated by the arrows.

1. Arrange the A squares in three rows of four squares each until you're happy with the placement. Don't stitch them yet.

2. To make the purse corners, layer a B square right sides together on top of the A square in the upper-left corner of your arrangement. Draw a diagonal line from corner to corner on the wrong side of the B square. Sew on the line, press, and trim the excess fabric, leaving a ¼" seam allowance. Repeat for the upper-right, lower-left, and lower-right corner squares. Replace the pieced squares back in your layout.

3. Sew the squares into rows and press. Join the rows and press. The unit should measure 4½" × 3½".

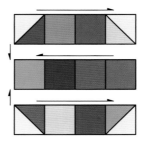

4. Sew C rectangles to the sides of the block and press. Sew the D rectangles to the top and bottom of the block and press.

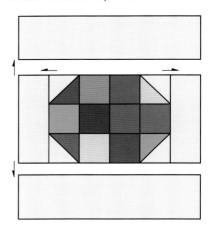

5. Sew the two buttons on the top of the purse block to create the "clasp."

Four Corner Spinwheel

• KIMBERLY EINMO •

My hectic but fun travel schedule is represented by the pinwheel in this block: I often feel like my life is spinning by in a whirl as I travel to teach. There are four triangles in the block corners which represent the four corners of the globe. I'm always happiest when I'm traveling and meeting quilters! ~Kimberly

What You'll Need

1 cream print piece, 8" × 10"; cut into:

A: 4 squares, 2" × 2"

B: 4 rectangles, 2" × 3½"

C: 4 dark brown print squares, 2" × 2"

D: 4 navy print rectangles, 2" × 3½"

E: 4 pink print squares, 2" × 2"

Assembly

Press all seam allowances in the directions indicated by the arrows.

1. Draw a diagonal line from corner to corner on the wrong side of the A, C, and E squares.

2. Place a C square right sides together with a B rectangle. Referring to "Stitch and Flip" on page 136, sew, press, and trim to make a rectangle unit with a triangle on one end. Make four units that measure 2" × 3½".

Make 4.

3. Using the stitch-and-flip technique, sew an A square on the right end of a D rectangle. Repeat on the left end with an E square. Make four units that measure 2" × 3½".

Make 4.

4. Arrange the units as shown. Sew them together in four groups of two and press. Sew the four groups together to create the block. Press.

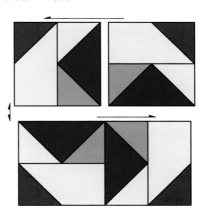

Center

• KATE SPAIN •

The methodical attention, care, and focus it takes to measure, cut, and sew fabric pieces together into a quilt is an activity that I enjoy more than I ever imagined. Work, deadlines, and the busyness of everyday life dissolve and I feel peaceful, centered, and happy. This block design is meant to reflect this feeling and all the tranquil moments I treasure at my sewing machine. ~Kate

What You'll Need

A: 1 light print square, 2¾" × 2¾"
1 white solid piece, 6" × 8";
    cut into:
    B: 4 squares, 1⅝" × 1⅝"
    C: 2 squares, 2½" × 2½"
D: 1 yellow print square, 2" × 2"
E: 4 light blue print squares,
    1¼" × 1¼"
F: 1 red print square, 4¼" × 4¼"
G: 4 red check squares, 2⅜" × 2⅜"
H: 2 navy print squares,
    2½" × 2½"

Assembly

Press all seam allowances in the directions indicated by the arrows.

1. Referring to "Fast Flying Geese" on page 135, make four flying-geese units with the A and B squares. The units should measure 1¼" × 2".

Make 4.

2. Arrange the four flying-geese units, the D square, and the E squares as shown. Sew the units into rows and press. Sew the rows together and press to make the block center. It should measure 3½" square.

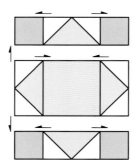

Referring to "Fast Flying Geese" on page 135

SLIM STITCHING

When using the Fast Flying Geese technique, sew a scant ¼" from the drawn line to compensate for the pressed seam and the stitching line. To reduce bulk in the seam, use a 50-weight thread when piecing.

~Jane

---

3. Repeat step 1 to make four flying-geese units with the F and G squares. The units should measure 2" × 3½".

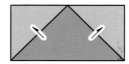

Make 4.

4. Draw a diagonal line from corner to corner on the wrong side of the C squares. Referring to "Triangle Squares" on page 135, layer the marked squares with the H squares to make four half-square-triangle units. Trim the units to 2" square.

Make 4.

5. Arrange the block center, flying-geese units, and half-square-triangle units into three rows. Sew the units into rows and press. Join the rows and press to complete the block.

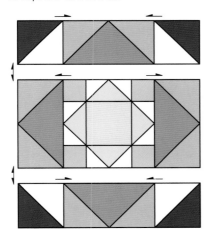

The alternating lights and darks in this version of the block create an almost telescoping effect as your eye moves between the tumble of squares and plus signs, working its way into the center light square.

Flights of Fancy

• JOANNA FIGUEROA •

For me, quilting and sewing is all about playing in the world of color. Before designing this block, I looked at the fabrics in my chosen palette and selected those that I wanted to work with. This block design showcases several different colors and fabrics without overwhelming any of them, creating a little bundle of loveliness. ~Joanna

What You'll Need

A: 2 white polka-dot squares, 3" × 3"

B: 2 yellow print squares, 3" × 3"

C: 8 white rectangles, 1½" × 2½"

1 green print piece, 2" × 10"; cut into:

    D: 4 squares, 1½" × 1½"

    E: 1 rectangle, 1½" × 2½"

1 blue print piece, 2" × 10"; cut into:

    F: 4 squares, 1½" × 1½"

    G: 1 rectangle, 1½" × 2½"

H: 6 navy print squares, 1½" × 1½"

I: 6 red print squares, 1½" × 1½"

Assembly

Press all seam allowances in the directions indicated by the arrows.

1. Draw a diagonal line from corner to corner on the wrong side of the A squares. Referring to "Triangle Squares" on page 135, layer an A square on a B square; sew, cut, and press. Make four half-square-triangle units and trim each to 2½" square.

Make 4.

2. Referring to "Stitch and Flip" on page 136, sew two D squares to a C rectangle to make a flying-geese unit. Make two. Repeat to make two of each color using F, H, and I squares. The units should measure 1½" × 2½".

Make 2 of each.

3. Repeat step 2 with the E and G rectangles and the remaining H and I squares to make two flying-geese units as shown.

Make 1 of each.

4. Arrange the half-square-triangle units and flying-geese units in rows as shown. Sew the flying-geese units in pairs and press. Sew the units into rows and press. Join the rows; press.

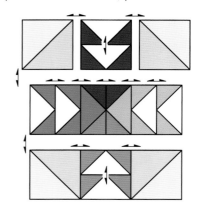

Starting Point

• LISSA ALEXANDER •

I'm a self-taught quilter, and often learn by doing things the wrong way. This block represents my hunger to start quilting 30 years ago; it begins in the middle and grows outwards. You never know how far one simple block can take you, and mistakes are the best way to learn, so don't be afraid to jump in and just get started! ~Lissa

What You'll Need

A: 12 assorted squares, 1½" × 1½"*

B: 4 gray print #1 rectangles, 1½" × 2½"

C: 4 gray print #2 rectangles, 1½" × 4½"

*Lissa used 3 red, 3 navy, 3 light blue, and 3 yellow squares and arranged them so each color radiates diagonally from the center.

Assembly

Press all seam allowances in the directions indicated by the arrows.

1. Sew four A squares together to make a four-patch unit for the block center. It should measure 2½" square.

2. Sew a B rectangle to two sides of the block center and press. Sew an A square to each end of the remaining B rectangles and press. Sew these to the top and bottom of the center unit; press. The unit should measure 4½" square.

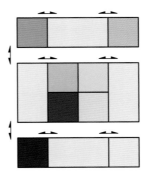

3. Sew a C rectangle to each side of the unit from step 2 and press. Sew an A square to each end of the remaining C rectangles and press. Sew these to the top and bottom to complete the block; press.

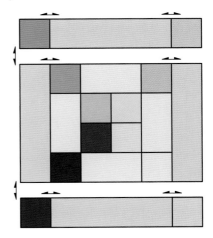

Hearts Aflutter

• PAT SLOAN •

I've been heart crazy for many years, so I designed this block to kick off the Splendid Sampler quilt-along, which started on Valentine's Day. Quilting has brought me amazing friends, incredible business opportunities, and adventures I never dreamed of. My heart truly is aflutter every time I see a quilt. ~Pat

What You'll Need

A: 2 light print squares, 3½" × 3½", for background

B: 2 light print squares, 3½" × 3½", for background

C: 4 red print squares, 1½" × 1½", for corners

D: 1 red print square, 5" × 5", for heart

Fusible web, 5" × 5"

Assembly

Press all seam allowances in the directions indicated by the arrows. The instructions are written for fusible appliqué. If you prefer hand appliqué, add a seam allowance to the heart pattern, which is on pattern sheet 1.

1. Alternating the A and B squares, sew them together to make a Four Patch block that measures 6½" square, including seam allowances. Press.

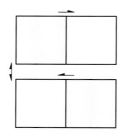

2. Draw a diagonal line from corner to corner on the wrong side of each C square. Referring to "Stitch and Flip" on page 136, place a marked square right sides together on each corner of the block. Sew, trim, and press.

3. Trace the heart pattern onto the fusible web. Cut out the heart about ¼" outside the marked line. Cut out the interior of the heart, leaving ¼" of fusible web on the inside of the line too. Fuse the heart onto the wrong side of the D square following the manufacturer's instructions.

4. Cut out the heart on the marked line and fuse it to the center of the Four Patch block. Stitch around the heart using a machine blanket stitch, if desired.

Happy Happy

• JEN KINGWELL •

This little block is all about the two things that make me incredibly happy: fabric and flowers. A vase of fresh flowers on my work desk brightens up any day. Use some of your favorite scraps to make a fresh fabric version that will be a sweet spot in any quilt. ~Jen

What You'll Need

1 light print square, 7" × 7", for background

1 plaid or print square, 4" × 4", for vase

Scraps of assorted prints for circles

Template plastic or freezer paper, 6" × 6"

Embroidery floss

Appliqué

Jen used needle-turn appliqué, and the instructions are written for that, but use your favorite method if you prefer. All the patterns are on pattern sheet 1. Reverse the vase pattern for fusible appliqué.

1. Fold the background square in half in both directions and press to crease. This marks the center and will help with positioning the vase.

2. Using the vase and circle patterns, trace one vase, four large circles, and five small ones onto your choice of template plastic or freezer paper. Cut out the shapes directly on the line. Use the templates to then cut one vase from the plaid and the nine circles from scraps, adding a seam allowance of approximately ¼" all around.

3. Position the vase and circles on the square, referring to the appliqué placement guide (above right) and photograph. Pin, baste, or glue the pieces to the background and appliqué in place.

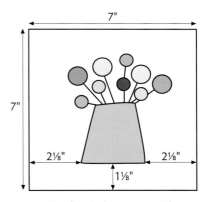

Appliqué placement guide

4. Embroider the stems using one strand of embroidery floss and a backstitch. See "Embroidery Stitches" on page 137 for stitch details. For bolder stems, use two strands of floss.

5. Press the block on the wrong side and trim it to 6½" square, keeping the design centered.

Flying High

• JANET CLARE •

My first fabric collection for Moda was called Hearty Good Wishes. It was inspired by my love of the coast in winter with its stormy waves, sea spray, and wild salty air. My feelings when seeing that fabric come to fruition were a little like these gulls soaring and flying high in the sky—that is to say, simply joyous. Hearty good wishes to you. ~Janet

What You'll Need

1 light print square, 7" × 7", for background

1 navy print piece, 4" × 8", for appliqués

Lightweight fusible web, 4" × 8"

Appliqué

The appliqué patterns are on pattern sheet 1. Instructions are written for fusible appliqué. If you prefer hand appliqué, reverse the patterns and add a seam allowance.

1. Trace the patterns onto fusible web, leaving ½" between shapes. Cut out the gulls, leaving about ¼" around each piece.

2. Carefully iron the fusible web onto the wrong side of the navy fabric, following the manufacturer's instructions.

Cut out the gulls on the traced lines. Remove the paper backing from each gull. You can use a pin to scratch the center of each gull, making the paper easier to peel off.

3. Position the gulls on the background square, referring to the appliqué placement guide and the photo. When you're happy with the placement, press in place.

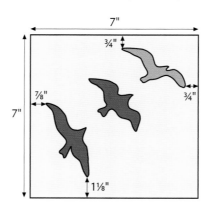

Appliqué placement guide

4. Stitch the edges of the appliqués by hand or machine. Janet used her machine drawing technique. To do this, set your machine for free-motion stitching by lowering the feed dogs and attaching a darning foot. Use matching or contrasting thread to stitch around the gulls, adding as much detail as you dare! For additional details on stitching options, see the "Sewing Tips" section of Janet's website: JanetClare.co.uk.

5. Press the block and trim it to 6½" square, keeping the design centered.

Sewing Machine

• PAT SLOAN •

The day I walked into Home Economics class in ninth grade and the teacher instructed us to "turn on the sewing machine," my life changed forever. I discovered a new skill, a new hobby, new friends, and ultimately a new life with my own design business. I've owned a sewing machine since ninth grade, and I can't thank my parents enough for buying me that first one! ~Pat

What You'll Need

1 light print square, 7" × 7", for background

1 black print piece, 4" × 6", for machine

Assorted scraps for the machine base, spool, fly wheel, heart, and circle

Lightweight fusible web, 6" × 8"

Embroidery floss or 12-weight Aurifil thread for needle

FABRIC SUGGESTION

Fussy cut a fun word print for the circle.

~Pat

Appliqué

The appliqué patterns are on pattern sheet 1. The instructions are written for fusible appliqué. If you prefer hand appliqué, reverse the patterns and add a seam allowance.

1. Trace the patterns onto the paper side of the fusible web, leaving ½" between the shapes. Cut out, leaving approximately ¼" around each piece.

2. Fuse the shapes to the wrong side of the chosen fabrics. Cut out on the traced line. Peel the backing paper away.

3. Position the sewing machine on the background square; place the base so that it butts up against the bottom of the machine. Add the spool, fly wheel, circle, and heart. Fuse in place following the manufacturer's instructions.

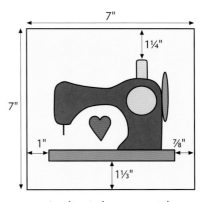

Appliqué placement guide

4. Using your favorite stitch, sew around the edges of the appliqués by hand or machine to secure them to the background. Pat used a machine blanket stitch.

5. Using 12-weight thread or two strands of embroidery floss, embroider the needle with a backstitch or outline stitch. Refer to "Embroidery Stitches" on page 137 as needed.

Sunday Best

• ANNE SUTTON •

When I began designing quilts, we lived in a small cottage-style house. My sewing room overlooked the garden. A bird feeder was just outside my window, and almost every morning a bunny came to visit, eating the seeds that the birds and squirrels tossed on the ground. He became the inspiration for many of my quilt designs, and I've featured him in this block, dressed in his Sunday best. ~Anne

What You'll Need

1 light print square, 7" × 7", for background

Assorted scraps for appliqués

Lightweight fusible web, 7" × 10"

Embroidery floss for nose, whiskers, eye, pocket, and flower stem

3 tiny buttons for jacket (optional)

Appliqué

The appliqué patterns are on pattern sheet 2. The instructions are written for fusible appliqué. If you prefer hand appliqué, reverse the patterns and add a seam allowance.

1. Trace the patterns onto the fusible web, leaving ½" between the pieces. Cut out the pieces, leaving about ¼" around each piece. Cut out the center of the grass, rabbit body, and jacket to minimize the layers of fusible web, leaving ¼" on the inside of the line.

2. Remove the paper backing and fuse each piece to the wrong side of the chosen scraps. Cut out on the drawn lines.

3. Arrange the pieces on the background square, referring to the photo. Fuse in place following the manufacturer's instructions.

4. Embroider the flower stem, whiskers, and pocket using two strands of floss and a backstitch or outline stitch. Embroider the eye and nose with a satin stitch. Add the buttons, embroider them using French knots, or leave them off if you prefer. Anne stitched around the jacket and the grass using a blanket stitch. Refer to "Embroidery Stitches" on page 137 as needed.

5. Press the block on the wrong side and trim it to 6½" square, keeping the design centered.

IT'S ALL YOURS

Personalize every quilt you make, even if you just embroider your initials or add a label. If your quilt has houses, embroider your address above one door. If your quilt has flowers, add a child's name to a petal. History is in the making with every quilt you create. Include the date!

~Anne

Sewing Nut

• FRANCES NEWCOMBE •

When I first discovered quilting, I fell in love with appliqué. My first appliqué quilt was a snowman quilt. I had a blast adding all the embellishments. This little squirrel block represents a delightful journey that brings out the joy of quilting. Just as the squirrel loves to stash nuts, so I stash my house full of fabrics! Use those decorative buttons that are packed away in your stash and have fun creating! ~Frances

What You'll Need

A: 1 light print rectangle, 6" × 7", for background

B: 1 green plaid rectangle, 1½" × 7", for grass

Assorted scraps for squirrel, tree, leaves, flower, and stem

Lightweight fusible web, 8" × 12"

Assorted buttons and charms (optional)

Assembly

The appliqué patterns are on pattern sheet 2. The instructions are written for fusible appliqué. If you prefer hand appliqué, reverse the patterns and add a seam allowance.

1. Trace the patterns onto the paper side of the fusible web, leaving ½" between the shapes. Cut around the shapes, approximately ¼" from the drawn lines.

2. Fuse the shapes to the wrong side of the chosen fabrics, following the manufacturer's instructions.

3. Cut out the shapes on the drawn lines and carefully peel off the paper.

4. Position the tree on the A rectangle and fuse it in place.

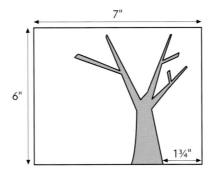

5. Sew the B rectangle to the bottom of A using a ¼" seam allowance. Press the seam allowances toward B.

6. Position and fuse the squirrel pieces, and then the leaves. Wait to fuse the nose and eye until all other pieces have been stitched to the block.

7. Stitch around the appliqués using your favorite stitch. Frances used a blanket stitch around the squirrel and a straight stitch on the tree and leaves.

8. Press the block from the wrong side and trim it to 6½" square. The grass should measure 1" from the raw edge to the seam.

9. Add embellishments and embroider details as desired. Frances added a small button for the squirrel's eye, a yo-yo flower with button center, and two acorn buttons. To make a yo-yo, cut a 3"-diameter circle and refer to "Yo-Yos" on page 136.

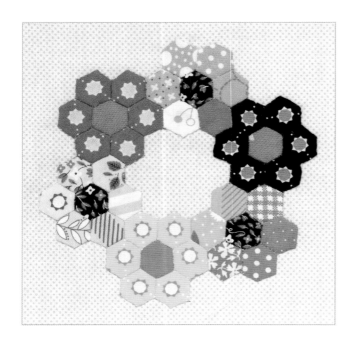

Inchy Hexagon Club

• JANE DAVIDSON •

Years ago I wanted to share my love of English paper piecing with the world, so I started the Inchy Hexagon Swap. Each month a fellow "hexaculturalist" would receive two hexagon flowers. This 6" block is a miniature version of the quilt block I made from all the hexagon flowers I received in that swap. ~Jane

What You'll Need

A: 7 assorted print squares, 5" × 5", for hexagons*

B: 1 light print square, 7" × 7", for background

Fabric glue stick or appliqué glue

White thread for basting and matching thread for appliqué

Note that Jane used scraps of the same color family for three of her flowers and she used two different fabrics for the flower centers. She also fussy cut the prints for three of her flowers. These instructions are for matching flower centers and matching hexagons in each flower.

Hexagon-Flower Preparation

1. Make a copy of the hexagon patterns on page 63 and carefully cut out 42 paper hexagons.

2. Glue six paper hexagons to the wrong side of each A square, allowing at least ¾" between each hexagon.

3. Cut around each hexagon, adding a ⅜" seam allowance.

4. Fold the edges of the fabric over the edge of the paper, mitering the corners. With a needle and thread, secure the miters with two backstitches. Fold the next edge over and take one long stitch to the next corner. Make sure that the fabric is folded firmly against the edge of the paper and secure the next corner.

5. Continue folding and stitching all the way around the paper template until you're back where you started. Take one backstitch and tie off. Cut the excess thread. Baste 42 hexagons.

Make 42.

HOLE IN ALL

Use a paper punch to make a hole in the center of each hexagon when preparing the foundation papers. Doing so will make it easier to remove the paper later using tweezers or a pin.

~Jane

6. Select one hexagon for the center and six for the petals. Using a very small whipstitch, sew one edge of each petal to the center hexagon, taking care to not sew through the paper. Start and finish each petal with a knot. Sew the petals together in the same way. Make six hexagon flowers.

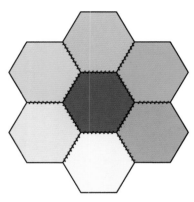

7. Lay out the six hexagon flowers in a wreath formation. Sew the flowers together. Starch and press well. Gently remove the papers, leaving the basting stitches in place.

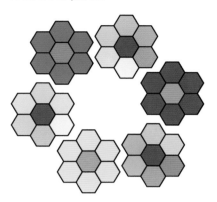

Assembly

1. Fold the B square in half in both directions and finger-press to mark the center.

2. Position the wreath in the center of the square. Secure with a glue stick or a few drops of appliqué glue and appliqué the wreath to the background by hand or machine.

3. Press the block carefully from the wrong side and trim to 6½" square, keeping the wreath centered.

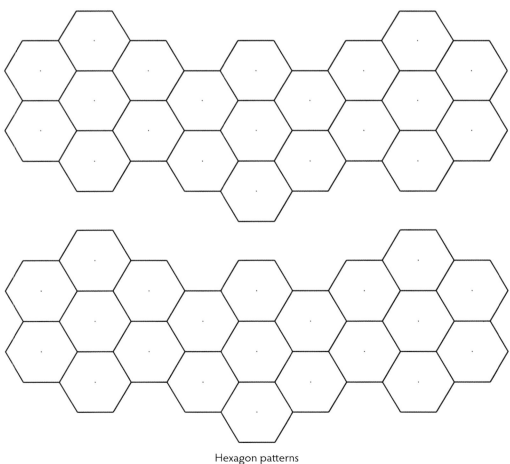

Hexagon patterns

Dreaming of Dresdens

• JANE DAVIDSON •

Dresden Plate is one of my favorite blocks. So many interesting possibilities emerge from the different layouts of the humble blade. ~Jane

What You'll Need

A: 1 light print square, 7" × 7", for background

B: 4 green print squares, 2½" × 2½", for blades

C: 4 red stripe squares, 2½" × 2½", for blades

D: 4 light print squares, 2½" × 2½", for blades

E: 1 black print square, 4" × 4", for center circle

F: 1 navy print strip, ½" × 10", for stems

G: 1 red print rectangle, 2" × 10", for small circles

Template plastic, freezer paper, spray starch, appliqué glue, and cotton swab or small brush

Dresden Plate Preparation

1. Make a template for the blade using the pattern on page 65 and template plastic. Trace the template three times onto the wrong side of each of the B, C, and D squares. Cut out along the marked lines.

2. Fold a blade in half lengthwise, right sides together. Finger-press to crease; sew a scant ¼" seam across the top. Carefully clip the top corner, leaving a few thread widths beyond the stitching line.

Trim.

Fold.

3. Finger-press the seam open. Turn to the right side; gently push out the point. Align the seam with the center crease and press flat. Make 12 Dresden blades.

Make 12.

4. Beginning at the center, sew the blades together in sets of three and press. Join two sets together to make a half circle; sew the halves together. Press.

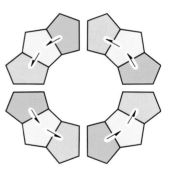

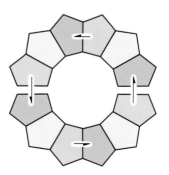

Stem Preparation

1. Heavily starch the F strip and press the strip in half lengthwise with wrong sides together.

2. Open the strip and press each long edge toward the center crease to make a ¼"-wide strip. Starch again and press.

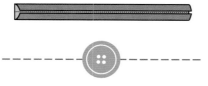

PRESSING PARTNERS

Use steam when pressing to set the folds in the strip and use a sewing stiletto or awl to hold down the seam ahead of the iron so you don't burn your fingers.

~ Jane

3. Cut the strip into six lengths, 1" long.

4. Position the stems on alternate wedges in the Dresden circle, referring to the photo on page 64, and glue or pin in place. Using matching thread, appliqué the stems by hand or machine.

Circle Preparation

1. Trace the large circle and six small circles onto the dull side of freezer paper. Cut out the circles on the traced lines. Press the large circle onto the wrong side of E and the small circles onto G, leaving at least ⅝" between them. Cut out the circles, adding a generous ¼" seam allowance.

2. Sew a gathering stitch (long running stitch) around the edge of the large circle on the right side of the fabric, about ⅛" in from the edge. Do not knot the start or end and leave a long thread tail at both ends.

3. Gently pull the thread tails to gather the fabric over the freezer-paper template until it's evenly gathered and taut around the edge of the circle. Smooth out any puckers on the edge. Tie off the threads to hold the gathering firmly in place. Repeat for the six small circles.

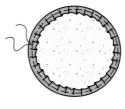

4. Spray starch into the lid of the spray can and use a small paint brush or cotton swab to apply it to the gathered seam. Using a medium-hot iron, press to secure the seam. Flip the circle over and press from the front.

5. Gently remove the freezer paper. Tighten the gathering stitches if required to reshape the circle. Repeat for each circle.

Assembly

1. Fold the A square in half in both directions and finger-press. Use the creases to center the Dresden circle on the background and glue or pin in place. Appliqué by hand or machine using a coordinating thread color.

2. Apply small dots of glue around the seam allowance of the large circle and position it on the Dresden circle. Using matching thread, appliqué it in place.

3. Repeat step 2 to appliqué the small circles to the Dresden blades above the stems.

4. Press the block from the wrong side and trim to 6½" square.

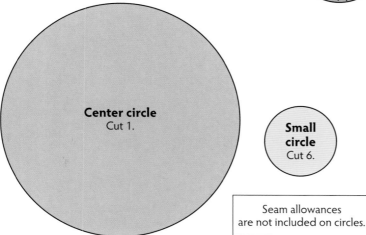

Center circle
Cut 1.

Small circle
Cut 6.

Seam allowances are not included on circles.

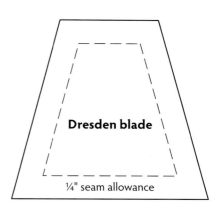

Dresden blade

¼" seam allowance

Sew South

• JENNIFER MATHIS •

Sew South is named for and inspired by the sewing retreat that I host. The center hexagon represents the retreat itself, where women come together to be inspired, relax, and have fun. Each individual hexagon petal represents the kind, creative, and talented individuals who attend. Together they make a lovely flower, which is only apparent when the shapes are combined. ~Jennifer

What You'll Need

A: 1 red print square, 7" × 7", for background

B: 6 black print squares, 3" × 3", for large hexagons

C: 1 blue print square, 3" × 3", for large center hexagon

D: 1 navy print square, 3" × 3", for small center hexagon

Template plastic, white cardstock, fabric glue stick, and spray starch (optional)

Assembly

1. Make a plastic template for each hexagon size using the patterns on page 67. Trace onto cardstock and cut out seven large hexagons and one small hexagon.

2. Trace a large hexagon onto the wrong side of each B and C square. Cut out, adding ¼" to ⅜" seam allowance all around. Repeat to cut one small hexagon from the D square.

3. Center the cardstock template on the wrong side of a fabric hexagon. Pin or use a dab of glue to secure the fabric to the template. Fold the edge of the fabric over the edge of the template. With a needle and thread, stitch through the fabric and cardstock. Fold the next edge over, securing the fold at the corner with a backstitch. Take one or two long stitches to the next corner. Make sure that the fabric is pulled firmly against the edge of the template. Fold the next edge and stitch the fold at the corner.

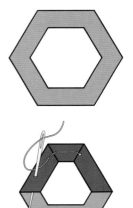

4. Continue folding and stitching all the way around the hexagon until you're back where you started. Take one backstitch and cut the excess thread. Repeat to baste the seven large hexagons and the one small hexagon.

5. Press the small hexagon well, using starch if desired. Remove the basting stitches and cardstock. Center it on the C hexagon and appliqué it in place by hand.

6. Press the remaining hexagons well and remove the basting stitches and cardstock.

7. Fold the A square in half in both directions and finger-press to mark the center.

8. Position the hexagons in a flower shape centered on the A square, leaving about ⅛" between the hexagons. Use a dab of glue to hold each hexagon in place. Let dry.

9. Appliqué each hexagon in place by hand or machine. Press the block from the wrong side and trim to 6½" square, keeping the design centered.

ALTERNATE COLORWAY

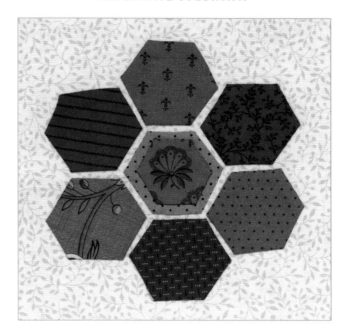

Why limit yourself to one fabric for your "petals" when you can ring the center hexagon with an assortment? Alternating between mediums and darks of one hue strikes just the right balance.

Small hexagon
Make 1.

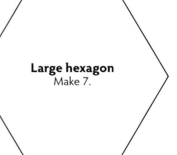

Large hexagon
Make 7.

The Constant Needle

• LAURIE SIMPSON •

There's never a moment that I don't have a stitching project in progress, whether it's hand piecing, hand appliqué, hand quilting, or embroidery. Handwork, like this hand-appliquéd flower, is calming and meditative. It's the way I was meant to work—always stitching, every day for the last 50 years. ~Laurie

What You'll Need

1 dark print square, 7" × 7", for background

1 pink print square, 5" × 5", for flower

1 red square, 4" × 4", for flower

1 gold print rectangle, 5" × 6", for stem and leaves

1 dark print square, 2" × 2", for flower center

Template plastic or freezer paper

Appliqué

The appliqué patterns are on pattern sheet 1. Laurie used needle-turn appliqué and the instructions are written for that method. The patterns are symmetrical and don't need to be reversed for fusible appliqué.

1. Make templates from plastic or freezer paper using the patterns.

2. Prepare the appliqué pieces by tracing around the templates on the right side of the chosen fabrics. Cut out, adding a scant ¼" seam allowance all around.

3. Place the stem in the corner of the background square; pin or glue baste in place. The stem is longer than needed to allow for trimming later. Appliqué the stem in place.

ELIMINATE SHADOWS

If you place a light appliqué over a dark or printed background, the background fabric might show through. To prevent that, make an appliqué shape of muslin or white solid. Place it on the background; then place your appliqué fabric over it.

~Pat

4. Position the outer petals over the top of the stem and appliqué in place. Position and appliqué the inner petals and then the flower center in place.

5. Place the leaves on each side of the stem and appliqué in place.

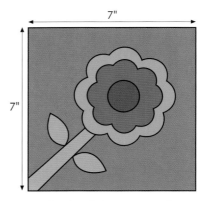

Appliqué placement guide

6. Press the block carefully from the wrong side and trim to 6½" square.

Summer's Gift

• KARLA EISENACH •

One of the many joys of summer is planting and caring for flowers. Flowers are truly a gift of the season. The colors of the flower in this block, set against a background of sunshine, will surely bring to mind your favorite blooms and cutting gardens. ~Karla

What You'll Need

A: 2 light yellow print squares, 4" × 4", for background

B: 2 yellow print squares, 4" × 4", for background

C: 1 green polka-dot rectangle, 4" × 8", for leaves and flower center

D: 1 red print square, 5" × 5", for ring of petals

Lightweight fusible web, 8" × 10"

Assembly

The appliqué patterns are on pattern sheet 1. The instructions are written for fusible appliqué. For hand appliqué, add a seam allowance to the flower patterns. The patterns are symmetrical and do not need to be reversed. Press all seam allowances in the directions indicated by the arrows.

1. Draw a diagonal line from corner to corner on the wrong side of the A squares. Referring to "Triangle Squares" on page 135, layer an A square with a B square, right sides together. Sew, cut, and press to make half-square-triangle units. Trim to 3½" square. Make four.

Make 4.

2. Sew the units together as shown to make a Pinwheel background that measures 6½" square.

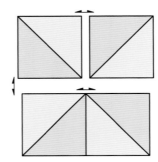

3. Trace the patterns onto the fusible web, leaving ½" between the shapes. Cut them out about ¼" outside the marked lines. Fuse the leaves and flower center onto the wrong side of the C square, following the manufacturer's instructions. Fuse the ring of petals to the wrong side of the D square.

4. Cut out the pieces on the marked lines and fuse them to the center of the Pinwheel block. Stitch around the pieces by hand or machine using a blanket stitch.

Appliqué placement guide.

Vintage Flower Basket

• PAM VIEIRA MCGINNIS •

There's nothing lovelier than an old piece of embroidery or a well-used quilt. I find vintage designs a constant source of inspiration. This block is based on an old heat-transfer embroidery pattern. While I love machine appliqué, these simple shapes could be easily hand appliquéd too. ~Pam

What You'll Need

1 navy print square, 7" × 7", for background

1 light print piece, 4" × 5", for basket

Assorted scraps for basket rim, leaves, and flowers

Lightweight fusible web, 8" × 12"

Jumbo rickrack, 8" long, for handle

Preparation

The appliqué patterns are on pattern sheet 1. The instructions are written for fusible appliqué. If you prefer hand appliqué, reverse the patterns and add a seam allowance.

1. Trace the patterns onto the paper side of the fusible web, leaving ½" between the shapes. Cut around the shapes, ¼" from the drawn lines.

2. Fuse the shapes to the wrong side of the chosen fabrics, following the manufacturer's instructions.

3. Cut out the shapes on the drawn lines and carefully peel off the paper.

Appliqué

1. Find the center of the background square by folding in half in both directions and finger-pressing a crease.

2. Center the basket on the background, ¾" from the bottom. Add the basket rim.

3. Slide one end of the rickrack under the rim and basket to form a handle. Keep the top of the handle ¾" from the top edge of the block. When you are pleased with the shape, trim the end of the rickrack and slide it under the rim and basket. Add a few dots of glue to hold the rickrack in place. Fuse the basket and rim.

4. Referring to the block photo, position and fuse the flowers and leaves, keeping the uppermost flower 1¼" from the top raw edge of the background.

5. Using threads that match the appliqué, machine blanket-stitch the appliqué shapes in place.

6. Using matching thread, straight stitch through the center of the rickrack.

7. Press and trim the block to 6½" square, keeping the design centered.

Pincushion Love

• PAT SLOAN •

No one in my family sewed, which means I didn't inherit a wonderful sewing basket from my mom, grandmother, or great-grandmother. But this didn't stop me from collecting vintage sewing notions. I'm drawn to anything used for sewing: old scissors, well-worn thimbles, and antique pincushions. ~Pat

What You'll Need

A: 2 light print squares, 3½" × 3½", for background

B: 2 light print squares, 3½" × 3½", for background

1 red print piece, 4" × 6", for pincushion

Assorted scraps for pincushion top, strawberry, and strawberry top

Lightweight fusible web, 4" × 12"

12-weight Aurifil thread or embroidery floss

2 tiny buttons or beads for pinheads

Assembly

The appliqué patterns are on pattern sheet 1. The instructions are written for fusible appliqué. If you prefer hand appliqué, reverse the patterns and add a seam allowance.

1. Sew the A and B squares together to make a Four Patch block. The block should measure 6½" square.

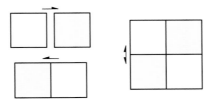

2. Trace the patterns for the pincushion, pincushion top, strawberry, and strawberry top onto the paper side of the fusible web, leaving ½" between the shapes. Cut around the shapes, ¼" from the drawn lines.

3. Fuse the shapes to the wrong side of the chosen fabrics, following the manufacturer's instructions.

4. Cut out the shapes on the drawn lines and carefully peel off the paper.

5. Position the appliqués on the background, referring to the photo for placement.

6. Fuse into place. Stitch around the edges by hand or machine using your favorite appliqué stitch. Pat used a machine blanket stitch.

7. Embroider the strawberry stem, pins, and lines on the pincushion using a stem stitch and 12-weight thread or two strands of embroidery floss. Refer to "Embroidery Stitches" (page 137) for details as needed.

8. Add a tiny button or a bead to the top of each pin.

Circle of Love

• GETA GRAMA •

I have three sisters who sew but aren't quilters. We got together and hand pieced a Grandmother's Flower Garden quilt for our mother. It took us a year and a half to sew together 3,300 hexagons. We all wish that we could freeze the time we spent together sewing, laughing, and eating cookies made by our mother. ~Geta

What You'll Need

1 white solid square, 7" × 7", for background

1 red print piece, 8" × 10", for appliqué

Lightweight fusible web, 8" × 10"

Water-soluble pen

TRACING TIP

When tracing onto fusible web, shade the drawing like the pattern diagram to keep track of which part is fabric and which is cut away.

~Pat

Appliqué

The appliqué patterns are on pattern sheet 2. The instructions are written for fusible appliqué. If you prefer hand appliqué, reverse the patterns and add a seam allowance.

1. Trace the pattern outline onto the background fabric using a water-soluble pen.

2. Trace pattern pieces 1–17 onto the paper side of the fusible web. You can keep the shapes fairly close together since they'll all be cut from the same fabric. Cut the group of shapes ¼" beyond the outer drawn lines.

3. Following the manufacturer's instructions, fuse the shapes to the wrong side of the red print.

4. Cut out the shapes on the drawn lines. Carefully peel off the paper backing from all the pieces.

5. Position the appliqué pieces on the background square in numerical order, referring to the photo. Add the center circle last.

6. Carefully fuse the pieces to the background.

7. Appliqué in place using your favorite appliqué stitch and matching thread.

8. Press from the wrong side and trim the block to 6½" square, keeping the design centered.

WORDS OF WISDOM

Don't say, "I can't" or "I don't like it" until you try it! Don't be afraid to break the rule."

~Geta

Fleur-de-Lei

• LYNN HARRIS •

Here, I combined the traditional Hawaiian appliqué technique of folding to create a pattern with the French fleur-de-lis motif. The mix makes it easy for me to daydream that I'm sitting on a beach in Hawaii or at a café in Paris, while I'm actually sitting at my daughter's dance studio or waiting for her during music lessons. ~Lynn

What You'll Need

1 dark print square, 7" × 7", for background

1 light print square, 7" × 7", for appliqué

Freezer paper or template plastic

Appliqué

The appliqué pattern is on pattern sheet 1. The instructions are written for needle-turn appliqué. The pattern is symmetrical and does not need to be reversed if you prefer to use fusible appliqué.

1. Complete the appliqué pattern by tracing it four times or by tracing it onto a folded piece of paper. Use the pattern to make a template from freezer paper or template plastic.

2. Prepare the appliqué piece by tracing around the template on the right side of the light square. Cut out, adding a scant ¼" seam allowance all around.

3. Fold the dark background square in quarters diagonally and press to make creases for placement.

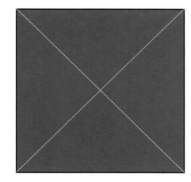

4. Using the creases, position and baste the appliqué to the center of the background fabric. Appliqué in place.

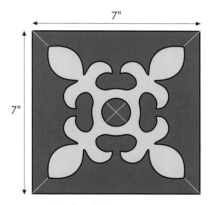

Appliqué placement guide.

5. Press the block carefully from the wrong side and trim to 6½" square, keeping the design centered.

Coneflower

• PAT SLOAN •

When I started my quilting design business, I was asked to submit ideas to quilting magazines. I was thrilled! One of my very first published projects was a coneflower pincushion. I never tire of adding coneflowers to projects and I've planted groupings of coneflowers throughout my garden. The colors range from pale pink to deep burgundy, but the purple ones are my favorites! ~Pat

What You'll Need

1 light print square, 7" × 7", for block background

Scraps of assorted prints for the petals, cone, and stem

Lightweight fusible web, 8" × 10"

Appliqué

The appliqué patterns are on pattern sheet 1. The instructions are written for fusible appliqué. If you prefer hand appliqué, reverse the patterns and add a seam allowance.

1. Trace the patterns onto the fusible web, leaving ½" between the shapes. Cut out the shapes, leaving about ¼" outside the drawn lines. Fuse the shapes to the wrong side of the selected scrap fabrics, following the manufacturer's instructions. Cut out the shapes on the drawn lines and peel away the paper backing.

2. Fold the background square in half diagonally and make a crease to help with placement of the flower and stem. Position the cone in the upper-right quarter of the background and arrange the petals under the cone. Slip the stem under the petals so it angles to the lower-left corner of the block. The stem end should fall within the outer seam allowance. Fuse in place.

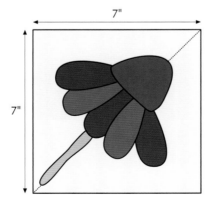

Appliqué placement guide.

3. Stitch around the shapes with a machine blanket stitch to secure the edges of the appliqués. Press the block on the wrong side and trim it to 6½" square, keeping the design centered.

TIPS FOR MACHINE APPLIQUÉ

To machine stitch around shapes with a blanket stitch, keep the straight part of the stitch on the background next to the shape, not on the shape, and don't leave a gap between the shape and the thread. For straight-stitch machine appliqué, stitch about ⅛" in from the shape's edge.

~Pat

Dedication Rose

• LISA BONGEAN •

I named my block Dedication Rose because I'm extremely dedicated to the art of quilting. I look forward to stitching every day. What I will create? Who will be in my class today? How can I do my best to inspire those who may be new to quilting or stitching? It brings me great joy to teach skills that may change someone's life. I can't comprehend a life without quilting in it! ~Lisa

What You'll Need

1 light print square, 7" × 7", for background

Scraps of assorted prints for flowers, leaves, and stems

Template plastic or freezer paper

Appliqué

The appliqué patterns are on pattern sheet 1. The instructions are written for hand appliqué. The patterns are symmetrical and do not need to be reversed if you prefer fusible appliqué.

1. Prepare the appliqués for your preferred method.

2. Fold the background square in half vertically, horizontally, and diagonally to create creases for easy appliqué placement. Position the pieces on the background fabric as shown and pin or baste in place. Stitch by hand using a blind stitch.

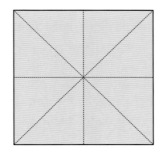

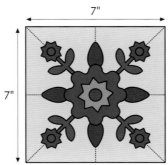

3. Press the block on the wrong side and trim it to 6½" square, keeping the design centered.

APPLIQUÉ YOUR WAY

If a block is hand appliquéd using the needle-turn technique, that's not the only way it can be done. Use any appliqué pattern, stitching method, or fabric. Use wool, flannels, velvet, and cottons. Blanket stitch, whipstitch, or stitch by hand or machine. Use 50-weight cotton thread or pearl cotton in various weights.

~Lisa

Cute as a Cupcake

• KIM CHRISTOPHERSON •

When I think of happy sewing memories, I can't help but think about times when I'm sewing with my girlfriends. There you'll find large stacks of fabric, a whole lot of laughs (maybe even a few tears), and definitely treats to be shared. And when that day involves friends and chocolate? Well, that's the icing on the cake! ~Kim

What You'll Need

1 light print square, 7" × 7", for background
1 light print piece, 4" × 3", for cupcake paper
1 brown print piece, 4" × 6", for icing
1 pink square, 3" × 3", for heart
Lightweight fusible web, 8" × 10"

Appliqué

The appliqué patterns are on pattern sheet 1. The instructions are written for fusible appliqué. If you prefer hand appliqué, add a seam allowance to the patterns. The patterns are symmetrical and do not need to be reversed.

1. Trace the patterns onto the fusible web, leaving ½" between the shapes. Cut out the shapes, leaving about ¼" outside the drawn lines. Fuse the shapes to the wrong side of the chosen fabric, following the manufacturer's instructions. Cut out the shapes on the drawn line and peel away the paper backing.

2. Position the cupcake paper, the icing, and the heart in the center of the background square. Fuse in place.

3. Stitch around the shapes with a machine blanket stitch to secure the edges of the appliqués. Press the block on the wrong side and trim it to 6½" square, keeping the design centered.

COLOR OUTSIDE THE LINES

Enjoy colors, pattern, scale, and texture! I rarely choose fabric from one line when making a quilt. Think outside the fabric lines. Choose one or two main prints; then go through the shop like a kid in a candy store, collecting colors, scales, and textures. You'll make an amazing quilt, I promise!

~Kim

At Home Anywhere

• JENNIFER KELTNER •

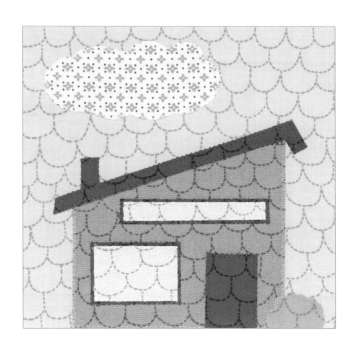

I've lived in five states and nine houses in my adult life. One of the first things I unpack when I move is my sewing machine. Whether I'm in a sewing studio or at the dining-room table, making a place to quilt is what turns a house into a home for me. It's where I make things I love for the people I love. ~Jennifer

What You'll Need

1 aqua print square, 7" × 7", for background

1 tan print square, 5" × 5", for house

1 red print piece, 5" × 6", for roof, window frames, chimney, and door

1 light print piece, 2" × 4", for cloud

1 white print square, 4" × 4", for windows

1 green print square, 2" × 2", for shrub

Lightweight fusible web, 9" × 12"

Appliqué

The appliqué patterns are on pattern sheet 1. The instructions are written for fusible appliqué. If you prefer hand appliqué, reverse the patterns as necessary and add a seam allowance.

1. Trace the patterns onto the fusible web, leaving ½" between the shapes. Cut out the shapes, leaving about ¼" outside the drawn lines. Fuse the shapes to the wrong side of the selected fabrics, following the manufacturer's instructions. Cut out the shapes on the drawn line and peel away the paper backing.

2. Referring to the photograph, position the pieces on the block background, keeping an extra ½" around the outer edges. Fuse the appliqués in place.

3. Using matching threads and a narrow machine zigzag stitch, sew around the outer edges of each appliqué shape. Jennifer used a zigzag stitch with a 2 mm width and a 1.4 mm length.

4. Press the block on the wrong side and trim it to 6½" square.

REDUCE STIFFNESS

To reduce bulk and stiffness in fusible appliqué, cut away the center portion of the fusible web for larger shapes, such as the house and cloud.

~Jennifer

Wild Rose

• PAT SLOAN •

My mom, Bonnie, doesn't sew or crochet or do any kind of crafty things. What we share is our love of flowers. Her favorite is a pink rose, so this design is for her. In my yard I have several rose bushes, pink for Mom and red for me. ~Pat

What You'll Need

1 white tone on tone square, 7" × 7", for background

Scraps of assorted prints for rose petals, ruffle, and center

Lightweight fusible web, 10" × 12"

Appliqué

The appliqué patterns are on pattern sheet 1. The instructions are written for fusible appliqué. If you prefer hand appliqué, reverse the patterns and add a seam allowance.

1. Trace the patterns onto the fusible web, leaving ½" between the shapes. Cut out the shapes, leaving about ¼" outside the drawn lines.

2. Fuse the shapes to the wrong side of the chosen fabrics, following the manufacturer's instructions. Cut out the shapes on the drawn line and peel away the paper backing.

3. Fold the background square in half vertically and horizontally to create creases to help with placement. Position the petals in the center, and then place the ruffle on top. Add the flower center and fuse in place.

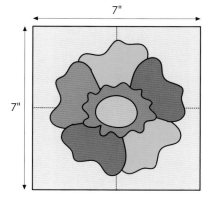

Appliqué placement guide

4. Stitch around the shapes with a machine blanket stitch to secure the edges of the appliqués. Press the block on the wrong side and trim it to 6½" square, keeping the design centered.

ONE SHAPE, ANY WAY

My appliqué is organic. For flowers, I repeat shapes. Instead of five different petals, I used one shape. How do I decide where to put them? The fabrics. Is it a bold floral? Put it on top. A tonal print? Underneath. I might have one side under and the other on top of the petal next to it. There's no right or wrong way.

~Pat

Skyscrapers

• STACEY LOWE •

Like many Australians, I love to travel to Japan. It's rich in culture and tradition, but it's also awesome for shopping! Tokyo has some amazing quilt shops tucked away in unexpected locations among the city's many skyscrapers. This block was inspired by my adventures in Tokyo, but can be translated to any city around the world. ~Stacey

What You'll Need

1 light print square, 7" × 7", for background

3 assorted navy print pieces, 4" × 7", for buildings

Lightweight fusible web, 8" × 10"

Appliqué

The pattern pieces are on pattern sheet 1. The instructions are written for fusible appliqué. If you prefer hand appliqué, add a seam allowance to the patterns.

1. Trace the patterns onto the paper side of the fusible web, leaving ½" between the shapes. Cut out the shapes, leaving approximately ¼" around each shape.

2. Fuse two building shapes to the wrong side of each of the fabrics, following the manufacturer's instructions. Cut out the buildings on the traced lines and carefully peel away the backing paper.

3. Position the buildings on the background, leaving a ½" margin along the bottom and side edges; fuse the appliqués in place.

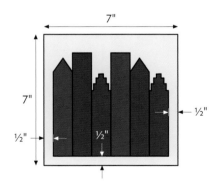

Appliqué placement guide

4. Blanket-stitch or straight stitch around the edges to secure the edges of the appliqués. Stacy used a machine straight stitch, two strands of thread, and a slightly longer than normal stitch. Press from the wrong side and trim the block to 6½" square, keeping the design centered.

Little Things

• JACQUELYNNE STEVES •

Whether it's noticing a flower on the side of the path, hearing a bird singing in the garden, or simply enjoying a leisurely cup of tea while savoring a favorite magazine, appreciating the little things makes life worthwhile. Yes, it's the accumulation of those beautiful little moments that build a happy life! ~Jacquelynne

What You'll Need

A: 12 assorted red and pink squares, 3⅛" × 3⅛", for patchwork

B: 1 cream square, 4" × 4", for background

Scraps of assorted blue and pink prints for appliqué

Lightweight fusible web, 4" × 4"

Assembly

Press all seam allowances in the directions indicated by the arrows. The instructions are written for fusible appliqué. If you prefer hand appliqué, reverse the patterns and add a seam allowance.

1. Pair up the A squares, using different fabrics in each pair. Place the squares right sides together and draw a line from corner to corner on the wrong side of the lighter square.

2. Referring to "Triangle Squares" on page 135, sew, cut, and press to make a total of 12 half-square-triangle units.

Make 12.

3. Pair two different half-square-triangle units and place them right sides together, aligning the seams. Draw a diagonal line from corner to corner on the wrong side of the units, perpendicular to the seams. Sew ¼" from both sides of the drawn line; cut and press to make two hourglass units. Make 12 units and trim them to 2" square.

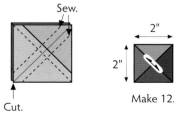

Sew.

Cut.

2"

2"

Make 12.

4. Join the units in two rows of four and two rows of two. Press.

Make 2.

Make 2.

5. Trace the appliqué patterns on page 81 onto the fusible web, leaving ½" between the shapes. Cut out the shapes, leaving about ¼" outside the drawn lines. Fuse the shapes to the wrong side of the chosen fabrics, following the manufacturer's instructions. Cut out the shapes on the drawn line and peel away the paper backing.

6. Arrange the appliqué pieces on the B square and fuse in place. Stitch the edges by machine using a zigzag or blanket stitch. Trim to 3½" square, keeping the design centered.

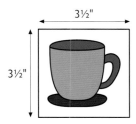

7. Sew the rows of two hourglass units to the sides of the appliquéd square and press. Sew the rows of four hourglass units to the top and bottom of the block. Press.

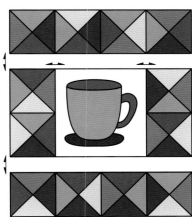

Do you and your friends swap mini quilts? This block is the perfect choice for a mini mug mat for each of your gal pals. Personalize each by pairing color choices with the recipient's favorite teas!

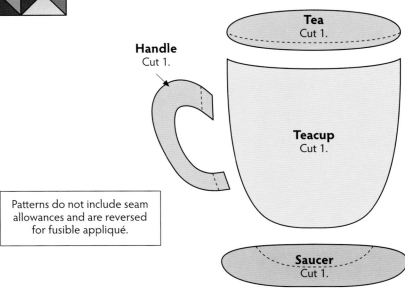

Tea
Cut 1.

Handle
Cut 1.

Teacup
Cut 1.

Saucer
Cut 1.

Patterns do not include seam allowances and are reversed for fusible appliqué.

Juggling

• LORENA URIARTE •

My happiest days are spent doing a little of everything I love. Often that means juggling family, work, and hobbies to get everything done. Fitting in all I want to do can leave me feeling a bit loopy at the end of the day. That's when I really enjoy some appliqué or handwork; it soothes my busy brain. How splendid! ~Lorena

What You'll Need

1 light print square, 7" × 7", for background

3 assorted print squares, 4½" × 4½", for balls

6 assorted print strips, ¾" × 5", for stripes on balls

3 navy print bias strips, ¾" × 8", for loops

Template plastic or freezer paper (Lorena used Templar, which is heat-resistant plastic)

⅛" bias press bar

Spray starch

Assembly

Press all seam allowances in the directions indicated by the arrows. The instructions are written for hand appliqué, but you can appliqué the balls and loops by machine if you prefer.

1. Cut across a 4½" square, approximately through the middle at an angle. Sew a ¾" × 5" strip between the two pieces and press. Cut the piece again in the opposite direction (Lorena made her second cut at a slight angle to create interest) and sew a second ¾" × 5" strip between the pieces. Press and grade the seam allowances (trim the seam allowances of the strip to approximately ⅛") to reduce bulk. Make three pieced units.

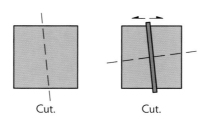

Cut.　　　　Cut.

Make 3.

2. Using the patterns on page 83, make three stiff circle templates from template plastic or several layers of freezer paper.

3. Place a circle template on each square and cut around it, adding a generous ¼" seam allowance. Sew a running stitch in the seam allowance around the template and draw up the thread to pull the circle tight around the template. Starch, press, allow to cool, and then remove the template.

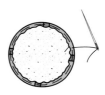

4. To make a loop, fold a ¾" × 8" bias strip wrong sides together and press. Stitch along the raw edges using a ⅛" seam allowance. Insert the bias bar into the tube and position the seam so that it's centered on one side. Starch, press, and allow to cool. Repeat for the two remaining bias strips.

Bias bar

5. Twist the bias strips around a pencil or wooden dowel to give them a curl; this will make it easier to create the small loops.

6. Position the circles on the background fabric and lightly draw the loops between them. Set the circles aside and arrange the bias strips into loops over the marked lines. Pin or baste them in position and appliqué them by hand or machine. Pin or baste the circles on the background and appliqué them in place. Starch lightly and press the block from the wrong side. Trim the block to 6½" square, keeping the design centered.

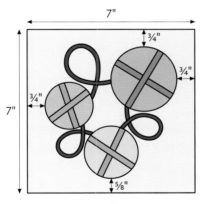

Appliqué
placement guide

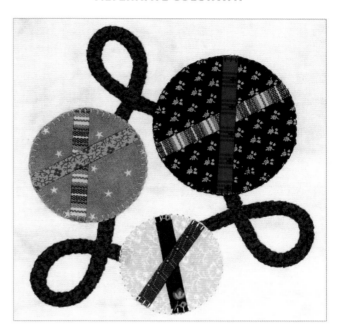

We all have a friend whose schedule is a constant juggling act. Why not finish this single block into a mini-quilt and affix it to the front of a journal or day planner as a gift?

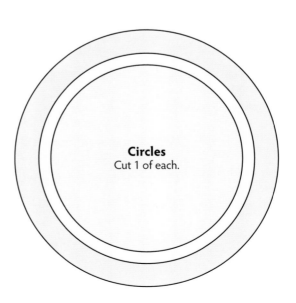

Circles
Cut 1 of each.

Double Bees

• BETH BRADLEY •

My grandma was a talented quilter who allowed me to start "helping" with her quilts when I was quite small. I share her love of sewing as well as her last name, so I decided to play off the idea of a quilting bee and a pair of quilting Bs (as in Bradley). Bees also symbolize hard work and sweetness—reminding me of my grandma and other quilters I've had the pleasure to know. ~Beth

What You'll Need

1 light print piece, 10" × 10", for background; cut into:

 A: 2 squares, 1½" × 1½"

 B: 2 squares, 2½" × 2½"

 C: 2 strips, 6½" × 2½"

D: 2 dark print squares, 1½" × 1½", for four-patch unit

Assorted scraps for bee bodies and wings

Lightweight fusible web, 8" × 10"

Embroidery floss and needle for embroidery (optional)

Removable fabric marker for embroidery (optional)

Assembly

Press all seam allowances in the directions indicated by the arrows. The instructions are written for fusible appliqué. If you prefer hand appliqué, add a seam allowance to the patterns.

1. Sew together the A and D squares as shown to make a four-patch unit. Press.

2. Orient the four-patch unit with the dark squares in the upper-left and lower-right corners. Sew the B squares to opposite sides of the four-patch unit to make the center strip. Press.

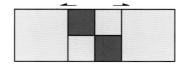

3. Sew the C rectangles to the top and bottom of the center strip. Press.

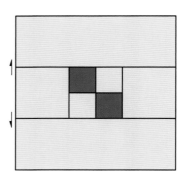

4. Trace the appliqué patterns on page 85 onto the fusible web, leaving ½" between the shapes. Cut out the shapes, leaving about ¼" outside the drawn lines. Fuse the shapes to the wrong side of the chosen fabrics, following the manufacturer's instructions. Cut out the shapes on the drawn line and peel away the paper backing.

5. Place the pieces on the block, referring to the photo for placement. Fuse in place. Stitch around each piece using a blanket or zigzag stitch to secure the edges. Press from the wrong side.

Optional Embroidery

To add a bit of movement to the block, use a removable marker or pencil to lightly draw a swirl next to each bee on the top and bottom strips, referring to the photo for inspiration. Use a backstitch or stem stitch to embroider along the drawn line.

SEE THE BEES

Fabrics with a small-scale print work best for the little bee pieces. To emphasize the bee theme, use a narrow stripe for the body pieces and cut them with the stripes running widthwise. Also, to allow the bees stand out, make sure the contrast is high between the dark and light fabrics.

~Beth

ALTERNATE COLORWAY

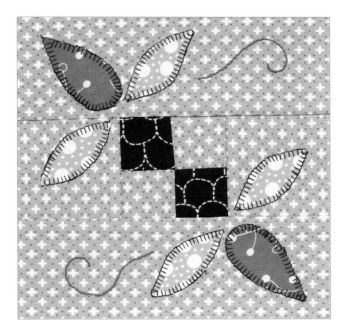

Turn your bees into rosebuds with a playful twist in color placement. Imagine the red embroidery is a sweep of a tendril. A single contrasting thread for the blanket stitching adds an extra pop overall.

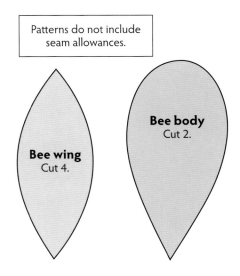

Patterns do not include seam allowances.

Bee wing
Cut 4.

Bee body
Cut 2.

In the Sunshine

• CHERYL ARKISON •

On sunny days, when flags blow in the breeze and I hear children playing outdoors, I take my sewing outside for a little handwork in the dappled light under a tree. This happy flag block encompasses so much of what I love about quilting right now—low-volume fabrics, some improv piecing, and hand appliqué. ~Cheryl

What You'll Need

A: 9 assorted print squares, 2½" × 2½", for background

B: 1 red print rectangle, approximately 3" × 6", for flag center

C: 2 navy print rectangles, approximately 3" × 6", for flag edges

Template plastic or freezer paper

Assembly

Press all seam allowances in the directions indicated by the arrows. The instructions are written for needle-turn or machine appliqué. Reverse the pattern for fusible appliqué.

1. Sew the A squares together in three rows of three to make a nine-patch unit. Press.

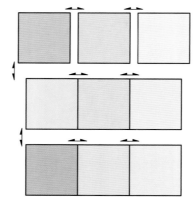

2. To cut the flag pieces, place the B rectangle on top of a C rectangle with right sides up; overlap them by about ¾". With scissors or a rotary cutter, cut a gradual, freehand curve lengthwise through both fabrics.

¾"

Cut.

3. Place the two pieces right sides together and sew the just-cut edge. Readjust the alignment of the cut edges every few stitches as needed. Focus on lining up the edges just in front of the needle. Be careful not to pull or stretch the fabric. Press.

4. Place the remaining C rectangle over the straight edge of the center fabric, again overlapping about ¾", and repeat the process to cut a gradual curve. Sew the pieces together as before and press.

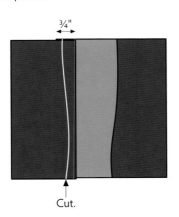

Cut.

5. Make a template for the flag using the pattern below and cut the shape from the pieced flag fabric, adding a seam allowance around the sides and bottom.

6. Position the flag on the background block, even with the top raw edge of the block, and appliqué it in place. Press the block from the wrong side.

PERMISSION TO PLAY

The best thing you can do for your quilting is play. We all know that kids benefit from the games and running around during recess and unstructured play; the same thing applies to quilting. Stop obsessing over perfection or getting it right. Just get in there, get your hands dirty, and play!

~Cheryl

Pattern includes seam allowance along top.

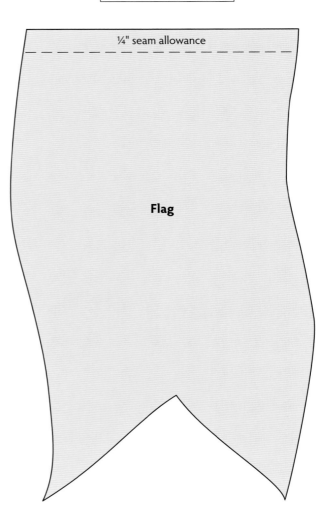

¼" seam allowance

Flag

Family Affair

• JANICE RYAN •

My mom taught me to sew when I was young and I have fond memories of that time spent with her. I've loved sewing ever since. Now that I have children, I enjoy seeing their excitement as we sew and create together. In this block, the X in three sizes symbolizes kisses and the love of sewing being passed down from mother to child to grandchild. ~Janice

What You'll Need

A: 8 green print rectangles, 1½" × 2", for piece #1

B: 8 red print rectangles, 2½" × 3", for piece #2

C: 8 light blue print rectangles, 1½" × 2½", for piece #3

D: 8 dark print rectangles, 1¼" × 5", for piece #4

E: 4 red polka-dot strips, 1¼" × 6", for center X

Paper for foundation piecing

Assembly

1. Make four copies each of the A and B patterns on pattern sheet 2. Paper piece them in numerical order, making sure to use the same print in the same spaces—fabric A for all the #1 spaces, fabric B for all the #2 spaces, and so on. Trim the excess fabric, leaving the ¼" seam allowance as indicated by the pattern. Do not remove the paper.

2. Fold the red polka-dot E strips in half with the short ends together and finger-press a crease to mark the centers. Matching center lines, sew an E strip to an A unit. Sew a B unit to the opposite side of the E strip, again matching the center lines. Press the seam allowances toward the E strip. Repeat to make four of these quadrants.

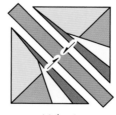

Make 4.

3. Using a ruler and rotary cutter, trim the E strip so it's even with the outer edge of the quadrant.

The quadrant should measure 3½" square. Repeat for all four quadrants; remove the papers.

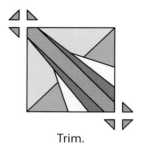

Trim.

4. Lay out the quadrants in two rows as shown and join. Press all seam allowances open.

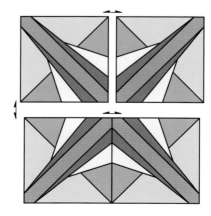

Goose on the Loose

· AMY SMART ·

I made this block with my four children in mind. When they were all little, I sometimes felt like I was running in four different directions, trying to keep up with each child's needs. Things felt wild, like a "goose on the loose." Sewing was my sanity—the thing that stayed done amid lots of repetitive tasks. ~Amy

What You'll Need

Yellow prints:

2 squares, 2¾" × 2¾", for piece #1; cut in half diagonally into 4 triangles (2 are extra)*

4 rectangles, 1½" × 2¼", for pieces #3 and #4

4 rectangles, 1½" × 3", for pieces #6 and #7

Green prints:

1 square, 2¾" × 2¾", for piece #1; cut in half diagonally into 2 triangles (1 is extra)

2 rectangles, 1½" × 2¼", for pieces #3 and #4

2 rectangles, 1½" × 3", for pieces #6 and #7

Navy prints:

1 square, 2¾" × 2¾", for piece #1; cut in half diagonally into 2 triangles (1 is extra)

2 rectangles, 1½" × 2¼", for pieces #3 and #4

2 rectangles, 1½" × 3", for pieces #6 and #7

Additional prints:

3 red print squares, 2¾" × 2¾", for pieces #2, #5, and #8; cut in half diagonally into 6 triangles (3 are extra)

3 light blue print squares, 2¾" × 2¾", for pieces #2, #5, and #8; cut in half diagonally into 6 triangles (3 are extra)

2 light print #1 squares, 2¾" × 2¾", for pieces #2, #5, and #8; cut in half diagonally to make 4 triangles (1 is extra)

2 light print #2 squares, 2¾" × 2¾", for pieces #2, #5, and #8; cut in half diagonally to make 4 triangles (1 is extra)

Paper for foundation piecing

You can use just 1 square cut in half diagonally for a less scrappy block without the extra triangles.

Assembly

1. Make four copies of the pattern on pattern sheet 2.

2. To piece a dark-geese block quarter, use yellow pieces and red triangles. Repeat with yellow pieces and light blue triangles to make a second block quarter.

3. Use navy pieces and one set of light triangles to make a light-geese block quarter. Repeat with green pieces and light triangles to make a second block quarter.

4. Join the quarters as shown and press carefully. Trim to 6½" square. Remove the foundation papers and press again.

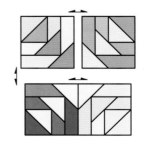

Stitching Fashion

• CHARISE RANDELL •

When I was a little girl my mom taught me how to sew by hand. That was my first experience sewing and I loved it. I spent hours with needle and thread making fashionable clothes for my dolls. Now decades later, my favorite thing to do is the same as when I was a wee one— sewing! ~Charise

What You'll Need

Extra fabric may be needed to match patterns or for fussy cutting motifs.

1 white solid fat eighth
  for background
1 dark print square, 10" × 10",
  for skirt (G1, H1, I1)
1 dark print square, 5" × 5",
  for bodice and straps
  (A1, B2, D1, E2)
1 red polka-dot piece, 1½" × 8",
  for skirt trim (G2, H2, I2)
1 red solid piece, 1½" × 4", for
  bodice trim (A2, D2)
1 gray print piece, 1½" × 6",
  for spool (J1, L1)
1 print or stripe piece, 2" × 3",
  for thread on spool (K1)
1 black solid piece, 1" × 5",
  for needle (M1)
Embroidery floss: red
Paper for foundation piecing

Assembly

1. Make one copy of each foundation pattern on pattern sheet 3. Charise prefers to leave the outer seam allowances off her paper foundations. This reduces bulk when joining sections together. If you want to use her method, trim the outer seam allowances from the paper and be sure to allow for the ¼" seam allowance all around. When sewing each section together, pin carefully and sew right next to the paper foundation.

2. Sew each section in numerical order, cutting fabric pieces as you go to fit the space. Be sure to preview the fabric to make sure it will cover the intended space. Trim and press each seam as you go. Sew sections A, B, D, E, and G–M.

3. Trim each section, leaving a ¼" seam allowance all around each piece.

4. Stitch section A to B, and then stitch A/B to C.

5. Stitch section D to E, and then stitch D/E to F.

6. Stitch A/B/C to D/E/F.

7. Stitch section G to H, and then stitch G/H to I.

8. Stitch A–F to G–I.

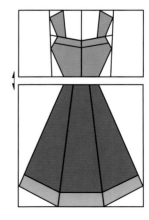

9. Stitch section J to K, and then stitch J/K to L.

10. Stitch J/K/L to M.

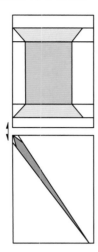

11. Stitch the dress section to the needle and thread section.

12. Transfer the thread design to the block using the embroidery pattern below. Carefully remove the foundation papers as needed and stitch the thread design with a backstitch. Refer to "Embroidery Stitches" on page 137 as needed.

ALTERNATE COLORWAY

One can only imagine the fun of creating an entire shop with dresses from every era on a quilt made with these blocks. Striped fabric makes variegated "thread" a reality in an instant!

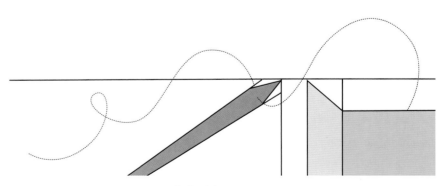

Embroidery pattern

Scrappy Happy Heart

• CHRISTA WATSON •

Quilting makes my heart sing, and I love using tons of fabrics in a piece. My philosophy is why use only one fabric when 20 will do? I also like the look of crazy-pieced patchwork in a structured block format. My Scrappy Happy Heart combines everything I love best about quilting. ~Christa

What You'll Need

1 white solid rectangle, 6" × 10"; cut into:

    1 rectangle, 2" × 3", for piece 1

    1 square, 2½" × 2½"; cut in half diagonally to make 2 triangles for pieces 8 and 15

    1 square, 5" × 5"; cut in half diagonally to make 2 triangles for pieces 19 and 20

Assorted scraps:

    6 rectangles, 2½" × 3½", for pieces 2–7

    6 rectangles, 2" × 6", for pieces 9–14

    3 rectangles, 2" × 5½", for pieces 16–18

Paper for foundation piecing

Assembly

1. Make one copy of the foundation pattern on pattern sheet 2.

2. Piece the block in numerical order, beginning with the white solid rectangle for piece 1. Trim and press each seam as a new piece is added.

3. When all pieces have been added, give your block a final pressing, and trim to 6½" square.

4. Carefully remove the foundation paper and press again.

PRESSING MAKES PERFECT

Because you're using lots of small, scrappy fabric bits and pieces in this block, you want the block to lie as flat as can be. Before adding the next piece, be sure to press each seam well. Keep your iron set up on a small pressing table within arm's reach. Also keep a small cutting mat and rotary cutter next to your machine. That way you can sew, trim, and press without ever having to get up or leave your workstation!

~Christa

Pencils

• JANE DAVIDSON •

I still remember the birthday when my aunty gave me a tin of 100 colored pencils. I think I used every color for every drawing I created back then. I wasn't afraid of color as a child, and I still continue the same eclectic style in my color choices today. ~Jane

What You'll Need

Assorted medium to dark prints:

    6 rectangles, 1½" × 4", for pieces A1, A3, B1, and B3

    3 rectangles, 1¾" × 4", for pieces A2 and B2

    3 rectangles, 1½" × 3", for pieces A4 and B4

    3 rectangles, 1¾" × 3", for pieces A6 and B7

3 brown print rectangles, 1¾" × 3", for pieces A5 and B6

1 light print piece, 10" × 10"; cut into:

    6 squares, 2½" × 2½", for pieces A7, A8, B8, and B9

    3 rectangles, 2" × 3", for pieces A9 and B5

Paper for foundation piecing

Assembly

1. Make two copies of the A foundation pattern and one copy of the B foundation pattern, both on pattern sheet 2.

2. Piece each section in numerical order. Trim and press each seam as a new piece is added.

3. Trim each section, leaving a ¼" seam allowance all around each section.

4. Stitch an A section to each side of the B section and press.

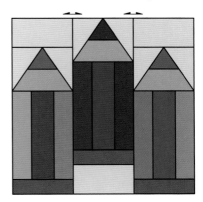

5. Carefully remove the foundation papers and press.

Selvage Saver

• PAT SLOAN •

Selvages—the alluring printed edges of fabric—are so prettily decorated with dots and sometimes cute images such as flowers or bunnies. The selvage tells us who designed and made the fabrics we love, and shows the colors used in the print. Many of us can't resist keeping them. I've dreamed of making a selvage quilt for a long time. This simple block is the beginning—want to join me? ~Pat

What You'll Need

8–10 assorted selvage strips*, 1¾" × 10"

1 muslin square, 7" × 7", for the foundation

Fabric glue (optional)

Paper for foundation piecing

Feel free to vary the number and width of strips.

Assembly

1. Arrange the selvage strips side by side in an order that's pleasing to you. This will determine the order of sewing. Keep in mind that the first and last strips will be in opposite corners and not much of the strip will show in the finished block.

2. Place the first strip on the upper-left corner of the muslin square so that the selvage edge is at the corner. Trim the excess

length from the strip and place the next selvage strip on top so that the selvage edge covers the raw edge of the first strip by about ¼". Trim the excess length if desired. Pin or use basting glue to hold the strips in place.

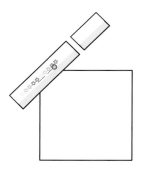

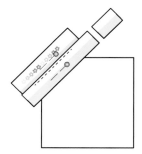

3. Sew the second strip close to the selvage edge through all layers. You're essentially topstitching the strips to the foundation.

4. Add a third strip in the same manner. Continue adding strips until the foundation is covered.

5. Press and then trim the block to 6½" square.

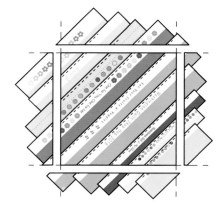

Balls in the Air

· AYLIN ÕZTŰRK ·

I love circles, and they're often the subjects of my designs or a prominent element in my quilts. From an early age, I engaged in ball sports, and now my life can only be described as keeping balls in the air with so many quilting projects underway all at once. ~Aylin

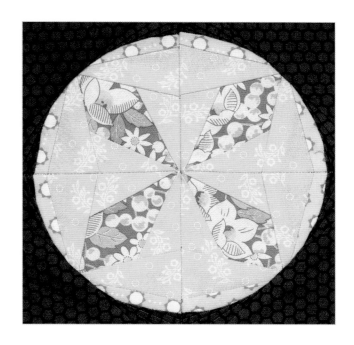

What You'll Need

4 red print rectangles, 2" × 3½", for piece 1

16 light yellow print rectangles, 2" × 3", for pieces 2, 3, 4, and 5

8 yellow print rectangles, 1" × 3", for pieces 6 and 7

1 navy print fat eighth; cut into:

    16 rectangles, 1" × 2", for pieces 8, 9, 12, and 13

    16 rectangles, 1" × 2½", for pieces 10, 11, 14, and 15

    2 squares, 4" × 4"; cut in half diagonally to make 4 triangles for piece 16

Paper for foundation piecing

Assembly

1. Make four copies of the pattern on pattern sheet 2.

2. Piece the block units in numerical order; trim and press each seam after sewing.

3. Trim the units to 3½" square.

4. Join the units together in pairs. Press the seam allowances open. Join the pairs and press.

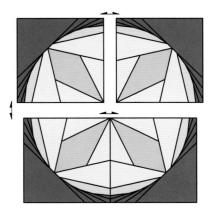

5. Remove the papers and press.

To join paper-piecing units, insert a pin vertically into the intersecting points on both pieces. Hold the papers together and keep the pin vertical so parts can't slide. Insert a pin through both units close to the vertical pin. Pin on the other side through the papers and fabrics to secure. Remove the vertical pin and repeat at all intersections.

~Aylin

Local Quilt Shop

• JANE DAVIDSON •

The local quilt shop is a quilter's home away from home. Shops are full of friendly faces ready to help us with all our quilting needs. I've designed a sweet quilt-shop block that includes the letter H for a happy, helpful home away from home. ~Jane

What You'll Need

1 tan print #1 square, 5" × 5"; cut into:

> 2 squares, 2" × 2", for pieces A1 and A3 (store front)
>
> 1 rectangle, 1¾" × 4", for piece A4 (store front)

2 dark brown print squares, 2" × 2", for pieces A2 and C2 (door and chimney)

1 tan print #2 rectangle, 1¼" × 4", for piece A5 (store front)

1 cream print rectangle, 2" × 4", for piece A6 (store front)

1 pink print rectangle, 6" × 8"; cut into:

> 2 rectangles, 2" × 4", for pieces A7 and B4 (store front)
>
> 1 square, 2" × 2", for piece B2 (store front)

2 beige print squares, 2" × 2", for pieces B1 and B3 (windows)

1 blue print rectangle, 6" × 9"; cut into:

> 1 rectangle, 2" × 4", for piece C1 (sky)
>
> 1 rectangle, 2" × 3", for piece C3 (sky)
>
> 1 square, 3½" × 3½"; cut in half diagonally for pieces D1 and D3 (sky)

1 brown print rectangle, 3" × 7", for piece D2 (roof)

Embroidery floss: red and black

Paper for foundation piecing

Assembly

1. Make one copy each of the foundation patterns for units A through D on pattern sheet 2.

2. Piece the block units in numerical order; trim and press each seam after sewing.

3. Trim each unit, leaving ¼" seam allowance all around each.

4. Join the A unit to the B unit. Press the seam allowances open. Join the C unit to the D unit and press. Join the A/B unit to the C/D unit. Press. Gently remove the papers and press again.

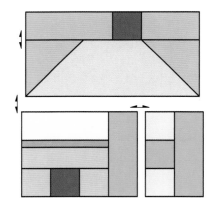

Finishing the Block

1. Trace the text onto the block using the embroidery pattern below.

2. Using two strands of floss, backstitch the words *Quilt* and *Shoppe*. Use a French knot to dot the *i*. Refer to "Embroidery Stitches" on page 137 as needed. Jane used red for *Quilt* and black for *Shoppe*.

3. Using one strand of floss, outline the word *Quilt* with cross-stitches.

PERSONALIZE IT!

Add embellishments such as decorative buttons or beads. You can also appliqué motifs or other text to add pizzazz to your block.

~ Jane

ALTERNATE COLORWAY

Novelty text prints may provide the perfect fussy-cutting opportunity, but let your imagination run wild as you create this block. What about a bakery, Santa's workshop, or a log cabin?

Whim

• FAITH JONES •

I have dual quilting personalities. I'm a planner who adores improvisational quilts. I designed this block to allow me to have the best of both worlds. Inspired by spontaneity in design, the block is assembled on a foundation using the paper-piecing technique. It gives off a definite improvisational vibe while still giving me control. ~Faith

What You'll Need

1 print rectangle, 3" × 5½", for piece 1

1 print rectangle, 4 ¼" × 6", for piece 2

1 print rectangle, 3½" × 4½", for piece 3

1 print rectangle, 2½" × 5 ¼", for piece 4

1 print rectangle, 3½" × 6½", for piece 5

1 print rectangle, 2½" × 4½", for piece 6

Paper for foundation piecing

Assembly

1. Make one copy of the foundation pattern on pattern sheet 2.

2. Piece the block in numerical order, beginning with piece 1 in the corner. Trim and press each seam as a new piece is added.

3. When all pieces have been added, give your block a final pressing and trim to 6½" square.

4. Carefully remove the foundation paper and press again.

A NOTE ON CUTTING

For foundation-paper-piecing patterns, the cut fabric sizes are the designer's recommendation. I always suggest sizes that are good for experts as well as beginners. To foundation paper piece a quilt, cut for just one block first. As you make it, decide whether to adjust the cut sizes. Cut fabric slightly larger than stated to give yourself a little more wiggle room.

~Faith

Shell

• JANE DAVIDSON •

I attended my first quilting class when I was 19. I drew a shell pattern, made templates that I cut by hand, and then pieced and quilted a queen-size quilt. Even then I wanted to make something that was completely my own design, and from that first simple shell, the passion for quilt design was ignited. ~Jane

What You'll Need

1 light print rectangle, 6" × 18"; cut into:

- 2 squares, 2½" × 2½", for pieces A1 and B1
- 4 rectangles, 2½" × 4½", for pieces A4, B4, C3, and D3
- 2 rectangles, 2" × 3¼", for pieces E3 and F3

Green prints:

- 2 rectangles, 1½" × 2½", for pieces A2 and B2
- 2 rectangles, 2" × 4", for pieces C1 and D1
- 2 rectangles, 3½" × 2", for pieces C2 and D2
- 2 rectangles, 2" × 4¼", for pieces E1 and F1
- 2 rectangles, 1¾" × 4¼", for pieces E2 and F2

Red prints:

- 4 rectangles, 2" × 3", for pieces A3, B3, C4, and D4
- 2 rectangles, 3" × 3½", for pieces E4 and F4

Paper for foundation piecing

Assembly

1. Make one copy of each foundation pattern on pattern sheet 3.

2. Sew each section A–F in numerical order. Trim and press each seam as a new piece is added.

3. Trim each section, leaving a ¼" seam allowance all around each section.

4. Stitch section A to C, and then stitch A/C to E. Stitch section B to D, and then stitch B/D to F. Sew the block halves together and press.

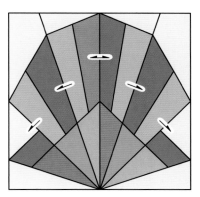

5. Carefully remove the foundation papers and press.

Homeward Bound

• KELLY LIDDLE •

I do all of my sewing during the weekends. I spend the drive home from work on Friday afternoons happily daydreaming about the projects I want to sew. I named my block Homeward Bound because flying-geese units are always at the top of that happy list. ~Kelly

What You'll Need

White solid fat eighth; cut into:

1 square, 3" × 3", for piece 1

6 rectangles, 1½" × 3", for pieces 3, 4, 6, 7, 9, and 10

2 rectangles, 2" × 3", for pieces 12 and 13

2 rectangles, 1½" × 3½", for pieces 15 and 16

1 square, 5½" × 5½"; cut in half diagonally to yield 2 triangles for pieces 17 and 18

Assorted scraps:

1 rectangle, 1½" × 2", for piece 2

3 rectangles, 2" × 3", for pieces 5, 8, and 11

1 rectangle, 2½" × 3½", for piece 14

Paper for foundation piecing

Assembly

1. Make one copy of the foundation pattern on pattern sheet 3.

2. Piece the block in numerical order, beginning with piece 1 in the corner. Trim and press each seam as a new piece is added.

3. When all pieces have been added, press the block and trim to 6½" square.

4. Carefully remove the foundation paper and press again.

STAY SEATED

Set up your sewing space for foundation paper piecing to speed up the process. I set up my mini ironing board next to my sewing machine, so I just swivel around in my chair to trim and press blocks. I use scissors instead of a rotary cutter to trim each seam. Saving a little time on each seam certainly adds up when you have 20 to 30 seams per block!

~Kelly

Stripes and Flowers

• SIOBHAN ROGERS •

Stripes and flowers are two of my favorite things. To create a sense of movement in this block, I used stripes in the background, which you could fussy cut so the stripes all align, if desired. I was inspired by the traditional Bear Claw and Sawtooth blocks—two more things I love. ~Siobhan

What You'll Need

Light blue stripe:

- 1 square, 4" × 4", for piece A1
- 8 squares, 2¼" × 2¼"; cut in half diagonally to make 16 triangles for pieces B2, B4, B8, B10, C3, C5, C9, and C11
- 1 square, 3¼" × 3¼"; cut into quarters diagonally to make 4 triangles for pieces B6 and C7
- 4 squares, 1½" × 1½", for pieces C1 and C13

Dark floral:

- 2 squares, 3½" × 3½"; cut in half diagonally to make 4 triangles for pieces A2, A3, A4, and A5
- 12 squares, 2¼" × 2¼"; cut in half diagonally to make 24 triangles for pieces B1, B3, B5, B7, B9, B11, C2, C4, C6, C8, C10, and C12

Paper for foundation piecing

Assembly

1. Make one copy of foundation pattern A and two copies each of B and C on pattern sheet 3.

2. Sew each section in numerical order starting with section A, the block center. Trim and press each seam as a new piece is added. Sew sections A, B, and C.

3. Trim each section, leaving a ¼" seam allowance all around each one.

4. Stitch the B sections to the top and bottom of A, and then stitch a section C to each side of the center unit. Make sure the pieces are oriented correctly. Press.

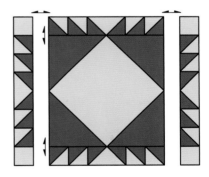

5. Carefully remove the foundation papers and press.

Bobbin Chase

• SCOTT HANSEN •

I designed Bobbin Chase just after my mother's death. I was in a very nostalgic mood, thinking back to the 1980s when I created counted cross-stitch projects. The four "bobbins" in Bobbin Chase are a nod to the cardboard winders I used to wind floss onto when I was stitching (akin to winding thread onto bobbins). ~Scott

What You'll Need

1 light print piece, 6" × 10"; cut into:
- 4 rectangles, 1½" × 2¼", for piece 1
- 4 squares, 2½" × 2½", for block corners

1 navy print piece, 10" × 10"; cut into:
- 4 rectangles, 1¼" × 1½", for piece 2
- 8 rectangles, 1¼" × 2½", for pieces 3 and 4
- 1 square, 2½" × 2½", for block center

2 different green print pieces, 2" × 10"; cut *each* into:
- 1 rectangle, 1½" × 2¼", for piece 5
- 2 rectangles, 1½" × 3¼", for pieces 6 and 7

2 different red print pieces, 2" × 10"; cut *each* into:
- 1 rectangle, 1½" × 2¼", for piece 5
- 2 rectangles, 1½" × 3¼", for pieces 6 and 7

Paper for foundation piecing

Assembly

1. Make four copies of the foundation pattern on pattern sheet 2.

2. Piece all four patterns in numerical order, beginning with piece 1 in the center. Use the same light print for each piece 1 and the navy print for pieces 2–4 in each one. Use a different red or green print for pieces 5–7 in each. Trim and press each seam as a new piece is added. Trim the pieced units to 2½" square and press.

Carefully remove the foundation paper and press again.

Make 1 of each.

3. Lay out the pieced units, the navy square, and four light 2½" squares as shown. Join the units into rows and press. Join the rows; press.

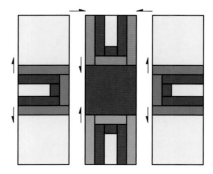

Bows

· JANE DAVIDSON ·

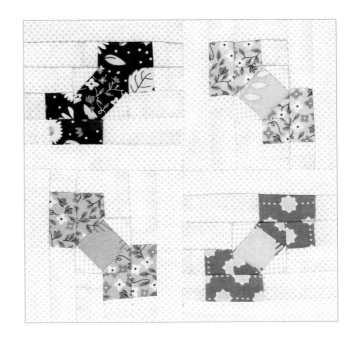

Some quiltmaking techniques are like learning to tie your shoelaces when you were little. Tying the perfect bow takes practice, patience, and perseverance. But with time, you'll be able to tie a bow—or paper piece four of them—in a snap! ~Jane

What You'll Need

1 white print piece, 12" × 20"; cut into:

    4 squares, 1¾" × 1¾"; cut in half diagonally to make 8 triangles for pieces A2 and A4

    8 squares, 1½" × 1½", for pieces B1 and C2

    8 rectangles, 1½" × 2", for pieces D2 and E1

    8 rectangles, 1½" × 3", for pieces D3 and E3

    8 rectangles, 1½" × 4", for pieces F and G

4 assorted print squares, 1¾" × 1¾", for pieces A1 (bow centers)

4 assorted prints, 5" × 5"; cut *each* into:

    1 square, 1¾" × 1¾"; cut in half diagonally to make 2 triangles for pieces A3 and A5

    2 squares, 1½" × 1½", for pieces B2 and C1

    2 rectangles, 1½" × 2", for pieces D1 and E2

Paper for foundation piecing

Assembly

1. Make four copies of the foundation patterns on pattern sheet 2.

2. Piece each bow pattern in numerical order, beginning with piece A1 in the center. Use matching print pieces for piece A3, A5, B2, C1, D1, and E2 in each bow. Trim and press each seam as a new piece is added.

3. Trim each unit, leaving ¼" all around. Join unit B to the right side of A and unit C to the left side of A. Add unit D to the top and unit E to the bottom. Press. Add the F and G rectangle to the sides. Press and trim the pieced units to 3½" square. Carefully remove the foundation paper and press again.

4. Lay out the bow units in two rows. Join the units into rows and press. Join the rows; press.

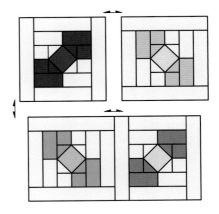

First Stitch

• KERRY GREEN •

I went to a progressive primary school where creative activities, especially sewing, were as much a part of our daily routine as reading, writing, and math. I still have my canvas sampler needlework book made when I was seven. The stitches were sewn in knitting yarn, including the cross-stitches that inspired this block! ~Kerry

What You'll Need

4 assorted dark print rectangles, 4" × 5"; cut *each* into:

    2 rectangles, 2" × 3", for pieces A1 and B1

4 light print squares, 3½" × 3½"; cut in quarters diagonally to yield 16 triangles for pieces A2, A3, B2, and B3

4 assorted dark print rectangles, 2" × 6", for piece A4

Paper for foundation piecing

Assembly

1. Make four copies of the foundation patterns on pattern sheet 2.

2. Piece the A and B patterns in numerical order, beginning with piece A1 or B1 in the corner. Use matching prints for piece A1 and B1 in each cross-stitch. Trim and press each seam as a new piece is added.

3. Leaving the paper in place, join the A section to the B section, matching the midpoints and ends. Carefully remove the foundation paper and press. Make four Cross-Stitch blocks.

Make 4.

4. Lay out the four blocks in two rows. The seams should nest together. Join the units into rows and press. Join the rows; press.

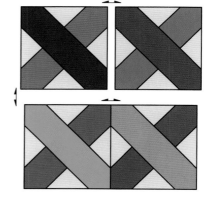

Spool

· MELANIE BARRETT ·

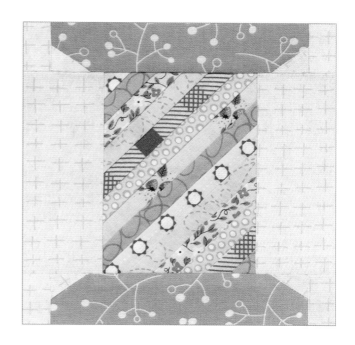

My earliest memories of sewing are with my great-grandmother. She was a very skilled seamstress who taught me to sew using her treadle machine. When I was 11, I had a paper route, and I used my tips and wages to buy a used Singer sewing machine. Since then, many other people have influenced me in the love of sewing and quilting, and they're all represented in the threads of this spool. ~Melanie

What You'll Need

2 taupe print rectangles, 2" × 6", for pieces A1 and B1

1 cream print piece, 10" × 10"; cut into:

  4 squares, 2" × 2", for pieces A2, A3, B2, and B3

  4 rectangles, 1½" × 2", for pieces A4, A5, B4, and B5

  2 rectangles, 2½" × 5", for pieces C15 and C16

7 assorted print strips, 1¼" × 8" to 12" long, for pieces C1–C14

Paper for foundation piecing

Assembly

1. Make one copy of each foundation pattern on pattern sheet 3.

2. Sew each section in numerical order starting with section A, the top of the spool. Trim and press each seam as a new piece is added. Sew sections A, B, and C.

3. Trim each section, leaving a ¼" seam allowance all around each one.

4. Stitch sections A and B to C and press. Carefully remove the foundation papers and press.

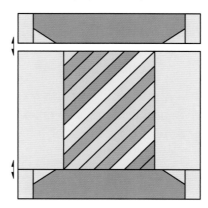

THREADS OF ADVICE

Instead of using a pin to position the first strip of fabric for the thread on the paper, I use double-sided tape. This way the paper lies flat when trimming and when adding the second piece of fabric. To make a quick block, use a striped fabric for the thread. Cut it so that the stripes run diagonally.

~Melanie

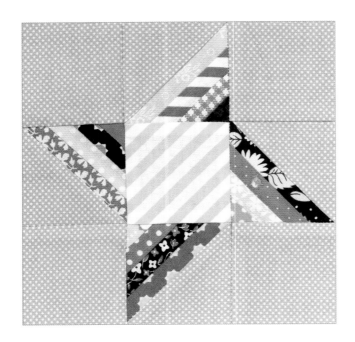

Heartstring Star

• ELIZABETH DACKSON •

I'm always drawn to scrappy quilts: quilts with lots of pieces and lots of stories. Scrappy quilts are like a fabric scrapbook for a quilter, with each fabric harkening back to some previous project or garment. Using some simple strings and a familiar star shape, you can create your very own little fabric scrapbook. ~Elizabeth

What You'll Need

1 light print piece, 7" × 10"; cut into:

2 squares, 3¼" × 3¼"; cut in half diagonally to make 4 triangles for piece 1

4 squares, 2½" × 2½", for block corners

4 assorted print rectangles, 1" × 4¼", for piece 2

4 assorted print rectangles, 1" × 4", for piece 3

4 assorted print rectangles, 1" × 3", for piece 4

4 assorted print rectangles, 1" × 2", for piece 5

1 stripe square, 2½" × 2½", for block center

Paper for foundation piecing

Assembly

1. Make four copies of the foundation pattern on pattern sheet 2.

2. Piece each pattern in numerical order, beginning with the light print for piece 1 in the corner. Trim and press each seam as a new piece is added. Trim the pieced units to 2½" square and press.

COLOR CUES

To keep track and stay organized when paper piecing a complex block, use colored pencils to color each section of the foundation.

~Jane

3. Lay out the pieced units with the four light squares and the striped square for the block center. Join the units into rows and press. Join the rows; press. Carefully remove the foundation papers and press again.

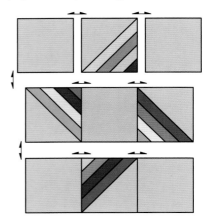

With Love From

• CAT DEMACK •

Much of my sewing is for giving away—projects for quilting bees, swaps, and gifts. I love the process of sewing for others: specially choosing the pattern and fabric; having the recipient on my mind as I cut, press, and sew; and finally popping it in the post or wrapping it up for giving. It's a privilege and a joy to be able to make for others with love. ~Cat

What You'll Need

1 navy tone on tone piece, 8" × 14"; cut into:

- 4 rectangles, 1¼" × 2", for pieces A1 and B1
- 2 rectangles, 1¼" × 3½", for piece A4
- 4 rectangles, 1¼" × 1½", for pieces C2 and C3
- 4 rectangles, 1¼" × 3", for pieces C6 and C8

1 light print piece, 10" × 12"; cut into:

- 2 squares, 4" × 4"; cut into quarters diagonally to make 8 triangles for pieces A2, A3, B2, and B3
- 2 squares, 1½" × 1½", for piece C1
- 4 squares, 2½" × 2½"; cut in half diagonally to make 8 triangles for pieces C4, C5, C7, and C9
- 1 rectangle, 2½" × 6½"
- 1 rectangle, 3" × 6½"

Paper for foundation piecing

Assembly

1. Make two copies each of the A, B, and C foundation patterns on pattern sheet 2.

2. Piece each A, B, and C pattern in numerical order. Trim and press each seam as a new piece is added. Leaving the paper in place, join the A and B sections together. Trim the pieced units to 2" square and press. Make two X blocks and two O blocks.

3. Arrange the X and O blocks in a row as shown and sew together. Press. Carefully remove the foundation papers and press.

4. Sew the smaller light rectangle to the top of the XO row and the larger rectangle to the bottom. Press.

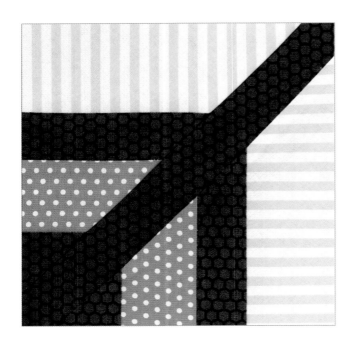

Flow

• LATIFAH SAAFIR •

Every now and then life blesses us with experiences where "flow" happens—that complete absorption in what we're doing. Quilting is like that for me. I often think about the first time I had an experience with flow and that was learning how to fly when I was 16. In just two weeks and with just 10 hours of flight time, I soloed in a Cessna 150. This block is inspired by that flight and the Cessna logo. ~Latifah

What You'll Need

2 light blue rectangles, 3" × 7", for pieces A1 and B1

1 navy tone on tone piece, 8" × 12"; cut into:

    2 rectangles, 2" × 5", for pieces A2 and B2

    2 squares, 2½" × 2½", for pieces A4 and B4

    1 rectangle, 2" × 10", for piece A5

2 red polka-dot rectangles, 2½" × 4", for pieces A3 and B3

Paper for foundation piecing

Assembly

1. Make one copy each of foundation patterns A and B on pattern sheet 3.

2. Sew each section in numerical order starting with section A. Trim and press each seam as a new piece is added.

3. Trim each section, leaving a ¼" seam allowance all around each one.

4. Stitch sections A to B. Press. Carefully remove the foundation papers and press again.

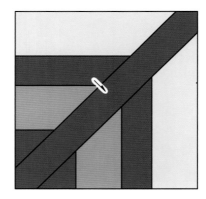

FABRIC OPTIONS

Your choice of lights and darks will change how the Flow block looks. To highlight the arrow or plane, use just two fabrics—a light and a dark—to make that image pop. Using a third fabric behind the wings creates interest. Or use a fabric that blends with the plane to add an arrow look. Latifah's stripe in the background gives the block lots of motion.

~Pat

Tiny Miracles

• APRIL ROSENTHAL •

I love being a quilter and a mom. I can't help but see a parallel between taking small pieces of fabric and creating something beautiful and helping tiny lives build themselves into the magnificent people they are meant to be. This block represents the miracles in my life—my children and the love, friendship, and joy quilting has brought me. ~April

What You'll Need

4 navy print #1 squares, 2" × 2", for piece A1

4 navy print #1 rectangles, 2½" × 3½", for piece B4

4 navy print #2 squares, 3" × 3", for piece A5

4 navy print #3 rectangles, 2½" × 3½", for piece A6

4 navy print #4 squares, 3" × 3", for piece B5

4 yellow print #1 squares, 2" × 2", for piece A2

4 yellow print #2 squares, 2½" × 2½", for piece A4

4 yellow print #3 pieces, 2" × 2½", for piece B1

4 yellow print #4 squares, 2½" × 2½", for piece B3

4 red print #1 rectangles, 1½" × 2½", for piece A3

4 red print #2 rectangles, 1½" × 2½", for piece B2

Paper for foundation piecing

Assembly

1. Make four copies each of the A and B foundation patterns on pattern sheet 2.

2. Piece each section in numerical order, beginning with the navy or yellow print for piece 1. Trim and press each seam as a new piece is added.

3. Trim each section, leaving a ¼" seam allowance all around each one.

4. Stitch section A to B and press. Make four block quarters.

5. Lay out the block quarters and join them into rows and press. Join the rows; press. Carefully remove the foundation papers and press again.

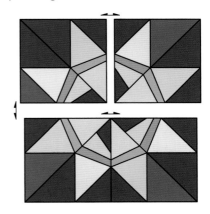

Shining Star

• JACKIE KUNKEL •

I had been sewing since sixth grade, making primarily garments, but it was my husband who got me into quilting. He encouraged me to get a hobby, so in 1993 I took a couple of quilting classes and fell in love. In honor of my husband, I made a star block—on our very first date, we sat and did quite a bit of stargazing. The sky was clear and the stars were twinkling. Let's all look to the stars! ~Jackie

What You'll Need

4 cream print #1 rectangles, 2" × 4", for piece A1

4 cream print #2 rectangles, 2" × 4", for piece B1

4 brown print #1 rectangles, 1½" × 2½", for piece A2

4 brown print #2 rectangles, 1½" × 2½", for piece B2

4 blue print #1 rectangles, 2" × 3", for piece A3

4 blue print #2 rectangles, 2" × 3", for piece B3

2 red print #1 rectangles, 2" × 3¼", for piece A4

2 red print #2 rectangles, 2" × 3¼", for piece A4

2 teal print rectangles, 2" × 2½", for piece A5

2 pink print rectangles, 2" × 2½", for piece A5

Paper for foundation piecing

Assembly

1. Make four copies each of foundation patterns A and B on page 111.

2. Piece each A pattern in numerical order, beginning with a cream print for piece A1. Trim and press each seam as a new piece is added. To help with correct color placement, piece all four of the A sections at the same time. You'll use the same cream, brown, and blue print in each section, but in two of the A sections, you'll use a different red print for piece A4. Pair the same red print with either a teal or pink print for piece A5. After adding the last piece, trim around the unit along the outer lines, which allows for a ¼" seam allowance all around.

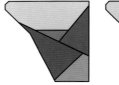

Make 2 of each.

3. Repeat the process for the B sections; use the same cream, brown, and blue print in all four sections.

Make 4.

4. Carefully remove the foundation papers and press the units again.

5. Place one A and one B unit right sides together. Using the finest pins that you have, pin where the seam will "bend" at the points of the A2, A4, and B2 pieces. Sew the seam, beginning with the dark prints, up to the pin and stop with the needle down. Remove the pin, lift the presser foot and pivot the piece to align the remaining edges. Finish sewing the seam and press. Repeat with the remaining units to make four block quarters.

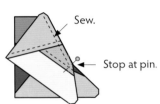

Sew.

Stop at pin.

6. Arrange and sew the four sections together and press.

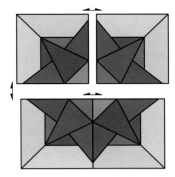

PIECING POINTER

When the A and B foundation sections are joined together, there's a slight jog in the seam. Place a pin there first and then pin at each end. Or use a glue pen just inside the seam allowances to keep them together while under the needle. Where you turn, stop with your needle down and pivot slightly. Complete the seam by sewing to the end.

~Jackie

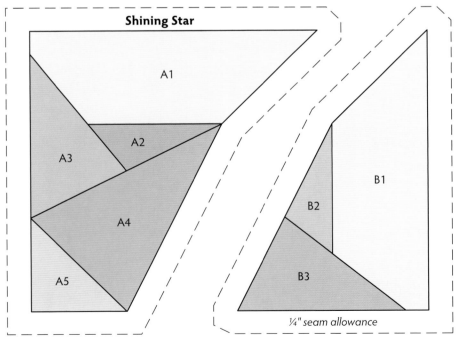

Shining Star

A1

A2

A3

A4

A5

B1

B2

B3

¼" seam allowance

Make 4 copies of each.

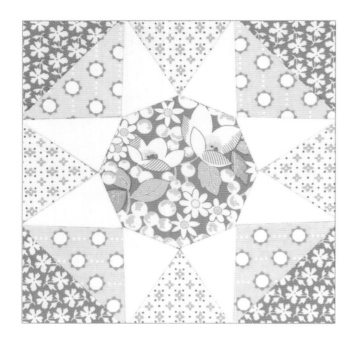

Under the Apple Tree

• BRIGITTE HEITLAND •

When patchwork was still just a hobby for me, I had a cozy dream. I would invite quilters into my garden and we would sit under the apple tree, sewing. Now the word apple *has even more importance—I sit in front of my Apple computer each day to create my designs, including this block. ~Brigitte*

What You'll Need

1 red floral square, 4" × 4", for piece A (octagon)

1 white tone-on-tone piece, 2½" × 20", for pieces B and Br

1 light blue print piece, 3" × 10", for piece C

1 yellow print piece, 3" × 12", for piece D

1 red print piece, 3" × 12", for piece E

Template plastic

Cardstock for English-paper-piecing foundations

Assembly

1. Make a template for pieces A–E using the patterns on page 113 and the template plastic. Trace around the templates onto the cardstock and cut out directly on the line to make the foundations.

2. Pin the shapes to the chosen fabrics as follows and cut out, adding a generous ¼" seam allowance all around for basting.

- Red floral: 1 of piece A
- White tone on tone: 4 each of pieces B and B reversed
- Light print: 4 of piece C
- Yellow print: 4 of piece D
- Red print: 4 of piece E

3. Referring to "English Paper Piecing" on page 134, fold the fabric seam allowances over the foundations and baste through all thicknesses.

NO-SEW OPTION

Save prep time by using a water-soluble glue stick to temporarily adhere the fabric to the paper templates. Put a hint of glue on the edge of the paper template and fold over the fabric so it tacks to the paper. To make glue-basted pieces, start with one side and then turn, fold over, do the next side, turn, and repeat all the way around the piece.

~Brigitte

4. Sew the B and B reverse triangles around the A octagon, placing them right sides together and using a whipstitch. Be sure to alternate the regular and the reversed shapes.

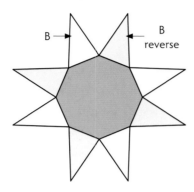

5. Sew the C and D shapes between the B star points, and then add an E triangle to each corner.

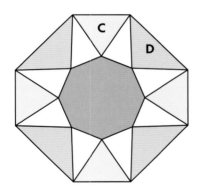

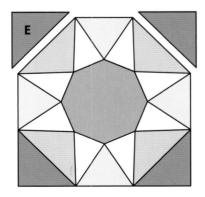

6. Clip the basting threads, gently remove the paper foundations, and press the block.

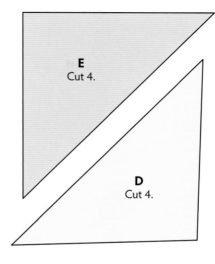

Patterns do not include seam allowances.

E
Cut 4.

D
Cut 4.

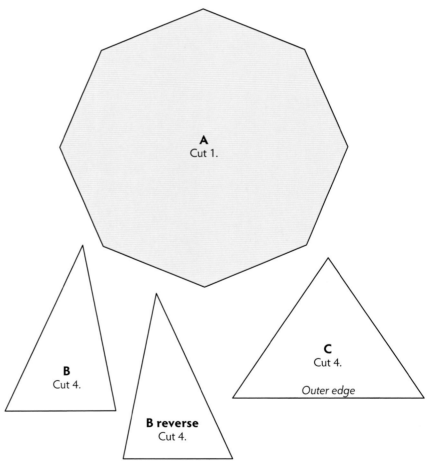

A
Cut 1.

B
Cut 4.

B reverse
Cut 4.

C
Cut 4.

Outer edge

Bee Happy

• KATJA MAREK •

Quilting and gardening are both essential aspects of my life. I especially like English paper piecing because I can do it anywhere, including sitting in my garden. When I moved into my home several years ago, it was new and there were no trees, flowers, birds, or bees. After much work and lots of planting, birds and bees moved in. Now I can sit in my garden and "bee" happy. ~Katja

What You'll Need

1 navy print square, 7½" × 7½", for background

1 blue print piece, 10" × 10", for pieces 1, 2, 4, 5, 8, 9, 19, 20, and 21

1 brown print square, 3" × 3", for piece 3

1 white print piece, 3" × 4", for piece 6 and hexagon flower center

1 cream print piece, 3" × 4", for piece 7

1 gold print piece, 4" × 6", for pieces 10, 12, 14, 16, and 18

1 black print piece, 4" × 6", for pieces 11, 13, 15, 17, and 22

1 red print square, 4" × 4", for hexagon flower

Cardstock for English-paper-piecing foundations

Spray starch or sizing

Fabric glue (optional)

Assembly

1. Use a photocopier to copy patterns 1–22 for the bee and the seven small hexagons for the hexagon flower using the patterns on page 115. Cut the pieces apart and trace around them onto stiff paper; cut out to make the foundations. Number each of the bee pieces for reference.

2. Pin the shapes to the chosen fabrics as follows and cut out, adding a generous ¼" seam allowance all around for basting.

- Blue print: 1 each of pieces 1, 2, 4, 5, 8, 9, 19, 20, and 21
- Brown print: 1 of piece 3
- White print: 1 of piece 6 and 1 hexagon
- Cream print: 1 of piece 7
- Gold print: 1 each of pieces 10, 12, 14, 16, and 18
- Black print: 1 each of pieces 11, 13, 15, 17, and 22
- Red print: 6 hexagons

3. Referring to "English Paper Piecing" on page 134, fold the fabric seam allowances over the foundations and baste through all thicknesses. Keep the piece numbers visible on the wrong side.

4. Whipstitch pieces 1–22 together in numerical order to create the large hexagon and bee tail. Sew pieces 10–20 together to make one unit before adding it to the head and wing units.

5. Press the hexagon bee carefully using spray starch or sizing to create nice crisp edges. Remove the basting threads and gently remove the paper foundations. If necessary, use a dab of fabric glue to hold tails and seam allowances in place.

6. Position the hexagon bee onto the navy background square and appliqué in place.

7. Whipstitch the small hexagons together to make the hexagon flower. Press and remove the basting stitches and papers.

8. Appliqué the hexagon flower to the block, below the bee's head.

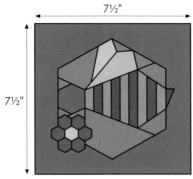

Appliqué placement guide

9. Press the block from the wrong side and trim to 6½" square so that the hexagon is centered side to side and the bee tail is ¼" from the right edge. It should just touch the seamline of the 6" finished square.

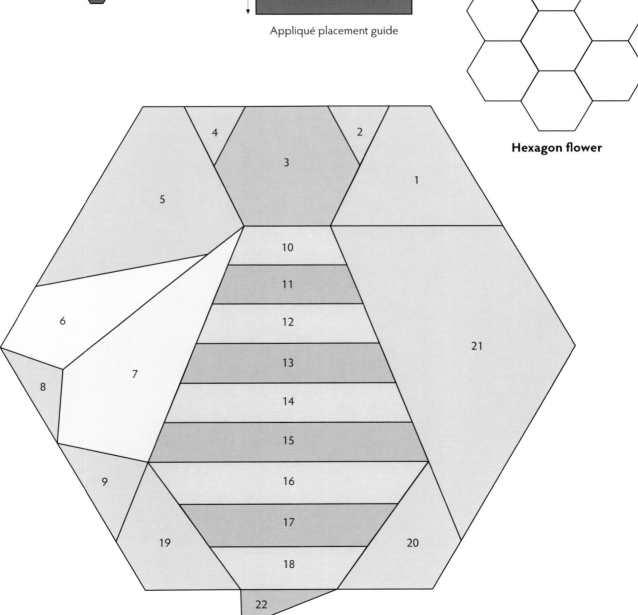

Hexagon flower

Hexagon bee

The Early Bird

• DESIGN BY JOAN FORD •

I'm a bird girl. I love birds! I also love the change in the seasons. Even so, I'm usually happy to see the cold, long winter end, naturally leading to splendid springtime. When I see the first robin, my heart sings! It means winter is over, days are getting longer, and warmer weather is within reach. Soon, I can stitch outside under a shady tree once again—my favorite quilty thing to do! ~Joan

To accommodate this book's space limitations, the authors have adapted the block construction to use paper-foundation piecing. For Joan Ford's traditional-piecing instructions, go to https://Hummingbird-Highway.com/TheEarlyBird.

What You'll Need

Directional fabrics are not recommended.

1 cream print piece, 9" × 21", for background; cut into:

- 1 rectangle, 1" × 6½", for piece A
- 1 square, 2⅛" × 2⅛"; cut in half diagonally to make 2 triangles for pieces B2 and E1
- 1 rectangle, 2" × 2½", for piece B4
- 1 square, 2½" × 2½"; cut in half diagonally to make 2 triangles for pieces C1 and H3
- 2 rectangles, 2½" × 3¾", for pieces C4 and F4
- 2 squares, 2⅝" × 2⅝"; cut in half diagonally to make 4 triangles for pieces D2, G4, G5, and H2
- 1 square, 1½" × 1½"; cut in half diagonally to make 2 triangles for piece D3 (1 is extra)
- 1 rectangle, 1¾" × 3¾", for piece D4
- 1 rectangle, 1½" × 2¾", for piece F1
- 1 rectangle, 1½" × 3½", for piece G1
- 1 rectangle, 1¾" × 2¼", for piece G6
- 1 rectangle, 1½" × 2¼", for piece H4

1 brown print #1 square, 2½" × 2½", for piece B1 (head)

1 red print piece, 6" × 8", for robin's breast; cut into:

- 1 square, 2⅛" × 2⅛"; cut in half diagonally to make 2 triangles for pieces B3 and C3
- 1 rectangle, 3½" × 3 ¾", for piece D1
- 1 square, 2½" × 2½"; cut in half diagonally to make 2 triangles for piece E3 (1 is extra)

1 gold print piece, 6" × 8", for beak, bottom, and legs; cut into:

- 1 square, 2⅛" × 2⅛"; cut in half diagonally to make 2 triangles for pieces C2 and E4
- 2 rectangles, 1" × 3½", for pieces G2 and G3

1 brown print #2 piece, 4" × 6", for wing; cut into:

  1 rectangle, 1¾" × 3", for piece E2

  1 rectangle, 1½" × 2½", for piece F2

1 brown print #3 piece, 4" × 6", for tail; cut into:

  1 square, 2" × 2"; cut in half diagonally to make 2 triangles for piece F3 (1 is extra)

  1 rectangle, 2" × 3½", for piece H1

1 black solid square, 1" × 1", for eye

Assembly

1. Make one copy of each foundation pattern A–H on pattern sheet 3.

2. Sew each section in numerical order starting with section B. Trim and press each seam as a new piece is added.

3. Trim each section, leaving a ¼" seam allowance all around each one.

4. Stitch section B to C. Press. Add section A to the top of B/C and press.

5. Stitch sections D, E, and F together and press.

6. Stitch sections G and H together and press.

7. Join the sections as shown and press. Carefully remove the foundation papers and press.

ALTERNATE COLORWAY

Dream up your very own winged wonder using whatever colorful mix makes your idea take flight. Rather than the red robin, it may be a plaid-breasted parakeet you conjure up in your imagination.

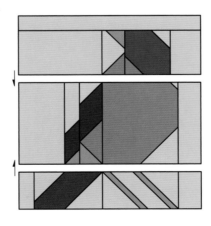

8. Trace the pattern for the bird's eye (below) onto the paper side of fusible web. Prepare the eye using the black square; fuse to the bird, referring to the photograph for placement. Secure the edge with a buttonhole, zigzag, or satin stitch.

Eye
Cut 1.

Appliqué pattern does not include seam allowances.

Stitch in the Garden

• GAIL PAN •

I love flowers, birds, and stitching. There's no better place to stitch than in the garden, surrounded by flowers and birds. This block combines appliqué and embroidery in a cute garden scene. ~Gail

What You'll Need

A: 1 beige print square, 7½" × 7½", for background

B: 2 brown print rectangles, 1" × 2¼", for the large spool

C: 1 red print rectangle, 1½" × 2¼", for the large spool

Assorted print scraps for small and medium spools

Embroidery floss: red, dark green, light green, taupe, yellow, blue, and purple

Template plastic and appliqué glue (optional)

Basic embroidery supplies (page 136)

Assembly

The instructions are written for needle-turn appliqué. If you prefer fusible appliqué, the pieces are symmetrical, so there's no need to reverse them. For embroidery techniques and stitch details, refer to "Embroidery Basics" on page 136.

1. Make templates for the three spools from template plastic using the patterns on pattern sheet 4.

2. To make the large spool, sew a B rectangle to the top and bottom of the C rectangle using a shorter than normal stitch length. Press. Place the large spool template over the unit so the dashed lines on the template align with the seams. Trace around the template and cut out, adding a ¼" seam allowance.

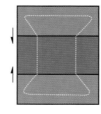

3. Trace the medium spool template and the small spool template onto the right side of the chosen scraps and cut out, adding a ¼" seam allowance.

4. Trace the embroidery design on pattern sheet 4 onto the center of the A square, but don't trace the spools.

5. Pin or glue the spools in place on the A square and appliqué in place.

6. Use two strands of embroidery floss to stitch the design according to the embroidery key. Refer to the photograph for color guidance.

7. Press the block on the wrong side and trim to 6½" square, keeping the design centered.

Snug as a Bug

• AMY SINIBALDI •

Sewing a quilt is an act of love. Every stitch is infused with love. Recently, I paused to admire my little girl sleeping under a quilt I'd just finished. I know I could have purchased a cute quilt for less money, but at that moment, with my girl and her stuffies all snuggled beneath her special quilt, I was so glad I'd made it myself. ~Amy

What You'll Need

1 light fabric square, 7" × 7",
    for background
Embroidery floss: black
Basic embroidery supplies
    (page 136)

Assembly

For embroidery techniques and stitch details, refer to "Embroidery Basics" on page 136.

1. Trace the pattern on pattern sheet 4 onto the fabric square.

2. Using two strands of floss, backstitch the lines as indicated in the pattern. You can stem stitch the design if you prefer.

3. Stitch a French knot for the eyes; use one strand of floss and a French knot for the teddy bear's nose.

4. Use one strand of floss to stitch the bunny's nose, the bear's muzzle, and the details on Baby's feet.

5. Trim the block to 6½" square, keeping the design centered.

ADD CHARM

My favorite way to make an embroidered piece look more like an ink illustration is to first stitch the entire pattern using two or three strands of floss. Then go back and randomly thicken some portions of the lines by adding more stitches, side by side.

~Amy

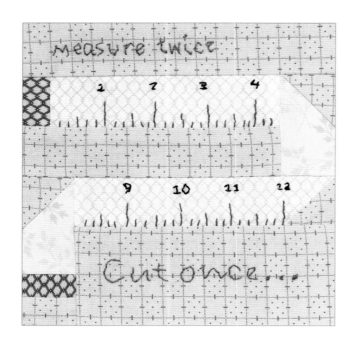

Measure Twice, Cut Once

• JANE DAVIDSON •

A woman in my first quilting group always said, "Measure twice, cut once." Sadly, she passed away, but I was lucky enough to inherit some sewing notions from her quilt room, one of which was a ruler. Every time I use that ruler her words still echo in my mind. ~Jane

What You'll Need

1 beige print square, 10" × 10", for background; cut into:

    A: 3 squares, 1½" × 1½"

    B: 1 rectangle, 1½" × 6½"

    C: 1 rectangle, 1½" × 5½"

    D: 1 rectangle, 2½" × 5½"

    E: 1 rectangle, 1" × 1½"

F: 2 cream print #1 rectangles, 1½" × 2½", for tape measure

1 cream print #2 rectangle, 4" × 7", for tape measure; cut into:

    G: 1 rectangle, 1½" × 5½"

    H: 1 rectangle, 1½" × 5"

I: 2 brown print rectangles, 1" × 1½", for tape-measure ends

Embroidery floss: blue, black, and red

Basic embroidery supplies (page 136)

Assembly

For embroidery techniques and stitch details, refer to "Embroidery Basics" on page 136.

TRANSFER TIP

For dark fabrics, use white or light grey carbon transfer paper to transfer the stitching designs. Be sure to place the fabric on a smooth, hard surface when tracing.

~Jane

1. Draw a diagonal line from corner to corner on the wrong side of the three A squares.

2. Place a marked square, right sides together, on the top edge of each F rectangle as shown, noting the direction of the diagonal line in each. Sew on the line. Trim to leave a ¼" seam allowance and press.

3. Place the remaining marked square, right sides together, on the end of the G rectangle as shown. Sew, trim, and press.

4. Sew the block together in sections as shown at right and press.

5. Using the patterns below, trace the letters, numbers, and ruler markings onto the block.

6. Using two strands of floss and a backstitch, embroider the block. Stitch French knots to dot the *i* in *twice* and add the ellipses after *once*.

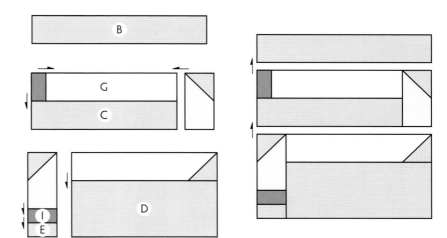

Embroidery Key

- • French knot

- —— Backstitch

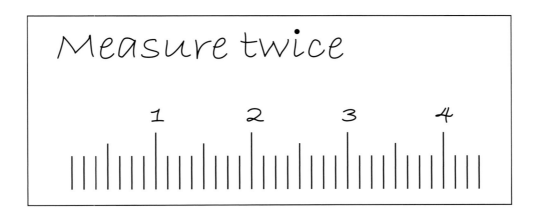

Measure Twice, Cut Once

Nature's Walk

• VICKI TUCEK •

Walking through a garden, park, or bush trail, I feel nature all around me. Tiny ladybugs and butterflies, attracted by the colors and nectar of the flowers, are always a pleasant surprise on my walks. Because nature is a mixture of all colors and textures, I've reflected this in the scrappy border of the block. ~Vicki

What You'll Need

A: 1 cream print square, 7½" × 7½", for background

B: 2 assorted print strips, 1" × 5½", for block border

C: 2 assorted print strips, 1" × 6½", for block border

D: 4 assorted print squares, 2½" × 2½", for block corners

Embroidery floss: yellow, pink, magenta, black, orange, light blue, dark blue, dark red, and green

Basic embroidery supplies (page 136)

Embroidery

For embroidery techniques and stitch details, refer to "Embroidery Basics" on page 136. Note that Vicki used a fine-point Pigma pen for tracing the design and she fused a stabilizer, such as Whisper Weft, to the wrong side of the background square. Use two strands of floss for all of the stitching.

1. Trace the design on page 123 onto the A square.

2. With the green floss, backstitch the leaves and vine, changing to satin stitch for the thicker areas of the vine.

3. With black floss, backstitch the butterfly antennae and satin stitch the body. Outline the wings with a backstitch in light blue and satin stitch the dots on the wings in dark blue.

4. Use yellow floss to backstitch the flower stamens and satin stitch the round ends. Satin stitch the flower centers using pink, orange, and magenta.

5. Satin stitch the sepals below the flowers with green.

6. For the ladybugs, satin stitch the bodies in red and black.

Use black floss to satin stitch the heads and backstitch the antennae. Make black French knots for the spots.

7. After stitching is complete, lightly press from the wrong side. Making sure the design is centered, trim the piece to 5½" × 5½".

Assembly

1. Sew a B strip to the top and bottom of the square and press. Sew a C strip to each side. Press.

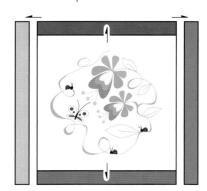

2. Draw a diagonal line on the wrong side of each D square and place one on each corner of the block square as shown. Sew on the lines and trim ¼" from the sewn line. Press.

 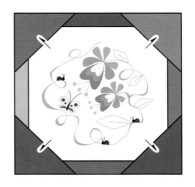

Embroidery Key

—— Backstitch

▨ Satin stitch

• French knot

Nature's Walk

The Wishful Garden

• KRISTYNE CZEPURYK •

While I consider myself a miserable failure as a gardener, embroidery offers me a creative outlet with almost always guaranteed success. I can stitch beautiful rows of flowers that don't require digging, watering, weeding, pruning, or staking! ~Kristyne

What You'll Need

A: 1 floral print #1 square, 5⅞" × 5⅞", for block background; cut into quarters diagonally to make 4 triangles

B: 4 white solid rectangles, 1½" × 4¾", for embroidery

C: 1 floral print #2 square, 1½" × 1½", for block center

Embroidery floss: dark green, dark pink, medium pink, light pink, light blue, medium blue

Basic embroidery supplies (page 136)

Assembly

For embroidery techniques and stitch details, refer to "Embroidery Basics" on page 136. Use one strand of floss for all of the stitching.

1. Arrange the A triangles, the B rectangles, and the C square as shown, right. Sew an A triangle to each side of a B rectangle and press. Make two units. Sew a B rectangle to each side of the C square. Press. Matching seams, sew the block rows together and trim the corners.

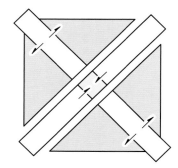

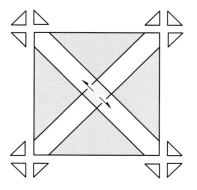

2. Trace the designs onto the white area of the block using the patterns on page 125.

3. Begin in the upper-left portion of the X, section A. Embroider a Cretan stitch with dark green, a lazy daisy stitch with light pink, and French knots with light blue.

4. In the upper-right portion of the X, section B, embroider a feather stitch in dark green, a straight stitch in light pink, a lazy daisy stitch in medium blue, and French knots in dark pink.

5. In the lower-left portion of the X, section C, embroider a fly stitch with dark green and French knots with medium blue.

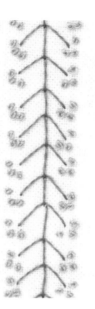

6. In the lower-right portion of the X, section D, embroider a herringbone stitch in dark green, a lazy daisy stitch with medium pink, and a straight stitch with dark pink. Press the piece carefully from the wrong side.

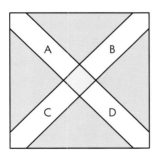

A   B   C   D

Embroidery Key

⌒   Lazy daisy

•   French knot

⋎⋎   Cretan stitch

⋗⋗   Feather stitch

—   Straight stitch

⟩⟩   Fly stitch

⋀⋀   Herringbone stitch

Blossoming

• JENNIFER REYNOLDS •

I first picked up a needle 10 years ago when a new friend gave me a few quilting and stitchery magazines. As my daughter and I browsed through them, I turned to her and said, "We can do this!" And we did! Those first months learning along with my daughter are now memories I treasure. We blossomed into lifelong stitchers and quilters. ~Jennifer

What You'll Need

1 light solid square, 7½" × 7½", for background

12-weight cotton thread or embroidery floss: green, turquoise, red, and blue

Embroidery floss: gold, brown, and green

Basic embroidery supplies (page 136)

Assembly

For embroidery techniques and stitch details, refer to "Embroidery Basics" on page 136.

1. Transfer the designs on pattern sheet 4 onto the fabric square.

2. Referring to the photograph for color guidance, backstitch the lines of the design according to the pattern key using 12-weight thread or two strands of floss. The exceptions to this are the needle and thread; backstitch those with one strand of floss.

3. Stitch cross-stitches where indicated.

4. Add running stitches where indicated on the pattern.

5. Satin stitch the centers of the daisies.

6. Chain stitch the button beneath the bird on the pincushion.

7. Sew French knot eyes on both birds, in the center of the lazy daisy flowers, and in the button.

8. Sew lazy daisy petals on the two book covers.

9. Press the block from the wrong side and, making sure the design is centered, trim the block to 6½" square.

GETTING STARTED

Don't have many floss colors? Take your background fabric to a needlework shop and choose six to eight colors that blend well.

If stitches in this design are new to you, trace sections of the pattern onto scrap fabric to practice. Sew a dozen lazy daisies, or practice sewing the words with a backstitch.

~Jennifer

Crocheted Thoughts

· ALYSSA THOMAS ·

I think of my grandma every time I make something. She was always busy crocheting doilies. In embroidery, the chain stitch looks very much like the crocheted version. So for this block, I embroidered a doily design using the chain stitch. I added an embroidered crochet hook in honor of my grandma! ~Alyssa

What You'll Need

A: 2 white solid squares, 2" × 2", for block corners

B: 2 red print squares, 2" × 2", for block corners

C: 1 white solid square, 4½" × 4½", for background

D: 4 assorted print rectangles, 1½" × 4½", for block border

Embroidery floss: variegated gold and gray or silver

Basic embroidery supplies (page 136)

Assembly

For embroidery techniques and stitch details, refer to "Embroidery Basics" on page 136.

1. Draw a diagonal line from corner to corner on the wrong side of the two A squares. Place them right sides together with the B squares and sew ¼" from both sides of the drawn line. Cut on the drawn line and press to make four half-square-triangle units for the block corners. Trim the units to 1½" square.

Make 4.

2. Arrange the half-square-triangle units, the C square, and the D rectangles into rows as shown. The light triangles should all point toward the center square. Sew the units into rows and press. Join the rows and press.

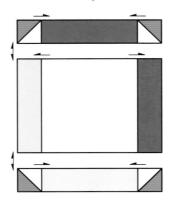

3. Trace the embroidery design on pattern sheet 4 to the center of the pieced block.

4. Using two strands of the gold variegated floss and a chain stitch, embroider the doily. Stitch the thread with a backstitch.

5. Use two strands of the silver or gray floss and a chain stitch to embroider the crochet-hook portion of the design.

6. Press the block gently from the wrong side.

Hearts and Flowers

· FIONA RANSLEY ·

Hearts and Flowers: because I love embroidery and my designs always seem to include flowers! My garden is a place where I find true inner peace and relaxation. I love spending time among the plants and drawing flowers for later stitching. Mother nature provides endless inspiration. ~Fiona

What You'll Need

1 light fabric square, 7" × 7", for background

Embroidery floss: red, aqua, and green

Basic embroidery supplies (page 136)

Embroidering the Block

For embroidery techniques and stitch details, refer to "Embroidery Basics" on page 136.

1. Trace the pattern on pattern sheet 4 onto the background fabric.

2. Using two strands of embroidery floss, stitch the design using the following stitches and floss colors.

- Heart: chain stitch in red
- Leaves and stems: backstitch in green
- Large flower centers: satin stitch in aqua
- Large flower shapes: backstitch in red and aqua
- Small flower petals: backstitch in aqua
- Small flower centers: satin stitch in red

3. Press the block from the wrong side and trim it to 6½" square, keeping the design centered.

SATIN STITCH SAVVY

For satin stitch, use a hoop. First backstitch around the section to be satin stitched. Then begin in the middle of the section and make long even stitches from one side to the other. For each stitch, go in on the same side and out on the same side. This gives a nice, even, flat satin stitch.

~Fiona

Stitch Crazy

• KATHY SCHMITZ •

Although I starting sewing on my mom's sewing machine at an early age, it's always been hand sewing and embroidery that have brought me the most joy. My hope is that this design—with its variety of embroidery stitches, the needle and thread, and a hand at "play"—brings joy to other fans of handwork and embroidery. ~Kathy

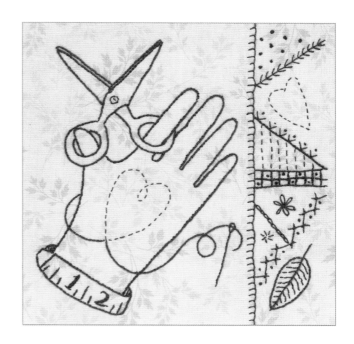

What You'll Need

1 light fabric square, 7" × 7", for background

12-weight cotton embroidery thread or embroidery floss: red

Basic embroidery supplies (page 136)

Embroidering the Block

For embroidery techniques and stitch details, refer to "Embroidery Basics" on page 136.

1. Trace the pattern on pattern sheet 4 onto the background fabric.

2. Embroider the design using one strand of 12-weight thread or two strands of embroidery floss. Stem stitch all the solid lines except the leaf veins and scissors screw. For those, use a backstitch. Refer to the pattern's embroidery key for other stitches.

3. Press the block from the wrong side and trim it to 6½" square, keeping the design centered.

MARKING, STITCHING, ENJOYING

The most important thing to me is to enjoy the process.

To transfer a design, I use freezer paper. Copy or trace onto the dull side of the paper; press the shiny side to the wrong side of your fabric. I use a FriXion pen to mark the design on the fabric. I do not use a backing fabric or hoop when stitching. Manipulating the fabric with both hands is satisfying.

~Kathy

Love Is the Answer

• PAT WYS •

Love brings peace and joy! Isn't that true? Many would also say that hand embroidery also brings peace and joy. This block, like all the other blocks in The Splendid Sampler, *is made with joyful celebration. Stitch and enjoy! ~Pat*

What You'll Need

1 light fabric square, 6" × 6", for background

2 different red print rectangles, 1" × 5½", for border

2 different red print rectangles, 1" × 6½", for border

Embroidery floss: red

Basic embroidery supplies (page 136)

Embroidering the Block

For embroidery techniques and stitch details, refer to "Embroidery Basics" on page 136.

1. Trace the pattern on pattern sheet 4 onto the background fabric.

2. Embroider the design using two strands of embroidery floss. Use the stem stitch for the solid lines and French knots for the birds' eyes.

3. Press the block gently from the wrong side and trim to 5½" square, keeping the design centered.

4. Sew red 1" × 5½" strips to the top and bottom of the embroidered block and press. Sew red 1" × 6½" strips to the sides of the block. Press.

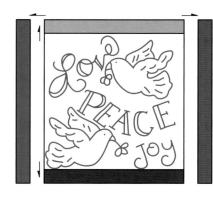

MAKE IT YOUR OWN

Put your own spin on this block by using some or all of the motifs and rearranging them as desired. How about stitching your name into the block?

~Pat

Gran's Button Jar

• LYNETTE ANDERSON •

I loved playing with my Gran's old buttons while she sewed clothing on her sewing machine. She taught me the names of wildflowers and animals, and my first embroidery stitches. I still have some of those early pieces of embroidery. I often think Gran would have loved to see how my handwork has improved! ~Lynette

What You'll Need

A: 1 cream square, 4½" × 4½", for background

8 assorted print pieces:

    B: 1 rectangle, 1" × 4½"

    C: 2 rectangles, 1" × 5"

    D: 2 rectangles, 1" × 5½"

    E: 2 rectangles, 1" × 6"

    F: 1 rectangle, 1" × 6½"

Assorted scraps for button jar and sewing machine appliqués

Template plastic or freezer paper

Embroidery floss: dark red, brown, black

Basic embroidery supplies (page 136)

Assembling the Block

The appliqué and embroidery patterns are on pattern sheet 4. The instructions are written for needle-turn appliqué. Reverse the patterns for fusible appliqué. Press all seam allowances in the directions indicated by the arrows. For embroidery techniques and stitch details, refer to "Embroidery Basics" on page 136.

1. Sew the rectangles to the A square, beginning with B and working alphabetically around the center square in a clockwise direction. Press after each addition.

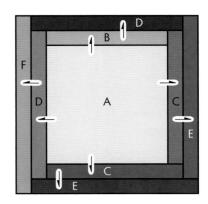

2. Make templates from plastic or freezer paper and prepare the button jar and sewing machine appliqués.

3. Using the photo as a guide, position the appliqué shapes on the A square. Pin or baste them in place. Stitch the appliqué shapes by hand using an appliqué stitch.

4. Trace the embroidery pattern onto the A square.

5. Embroider the design using two strands of embroidery floss. Refer to the block photo for colors and the pattern for stitching. Use backstitches, satin stitches, cross-stitches, running stitches, and French knots.

6. Press the block gently from the wrong side after the embroidery is complete.

If the construction techniques used in the blocks are unfamiliar to you, here you'll find the basic information you need.

Appliqué

The instructions for each block state the appliqué method used by the designer. To convert between fusible and needle-turn appliqué, you may need to reverse the patterns. Seam allowances are not included on the appliqué patterns unless noted. You'll need to add them for needle-turn appliqué patterns.

For machine appliqué, use a stabilizer on the back to support dense machine stitching (such as satin stitching) and to keep the fabric from tunneling. Choose a stabilizer that matches the weight of the fabric. After the appliqué is complete, gently remove the stabilizer.

FUSIBLE APPLIQUÉ

Raw-edged appliqué using paper-backed fusible web is a fast and easy way to appliqué. Because appliqué designs are drawn on the paper side of the fusible web, and then flipped when ironed onto the fabric, you may need to reverse the appliqué patterns prior to tracing the designs. (We have indicated where patterns have already been reversed.) Add ¼" underlap allowance to those edges that lie under another appliqué shape.

Trace the pattern pieces, also drawing the needed underlap allowances, on the paper side of the fusible web, leaving at least ½" between all the pieces. Cut about ¼" outside each drawn line.

To eliminate stiffness in pieces larger than 1", you can cut out the center of the fusible web ¼" inside the drawn line, making a ring of fusible web.

Following the manufacturer's directions, iron the web, paper side up, to the wrong side of the fabric. Cut out the shape exactly on the drawn line. Carefully

pull away the paper backing. Fuse the pieces to the background as shown in the placement diagram for the block you're making.

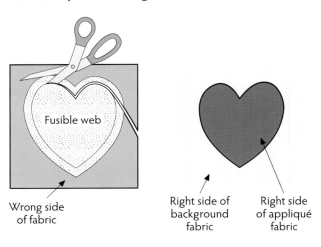

Wrong side of fabric

Right side of background fabric

Right side of appliqué fabric

To finish the raw edges, stitch by machine using a satin stitch, zigzag stitch, or blanket stitch and matching or invisible thread.

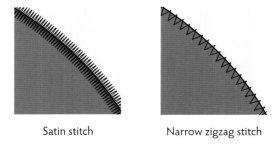

Satin stitch

Narrow zigzag stitch

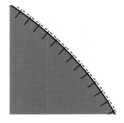

Blanket stitch

You can also stitch by hand using a blanket stitch.

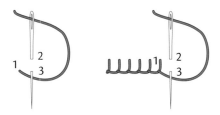

Blanket stitch

NEEDLE-TURN APPLIQUÉ

For this method of appliqué, it's helpful to cut your appliqué pieces so the bias edges are on the perimeter. This makes the edges easier to turn under and stitch smoothly in place. Trace the pattern onto freezer paper or template plastic and cut on the drawn line to make a template. Place the template face up on the right side of the fabric and lightly draw around it (place the template face down on the right side to reverse the appliqué). Cut out each appliqué about ¼" outside the marked line.

Pin or baste the appliqués on the background fabric. Stitch in place, using your needle to turn under the seam allowances as you stitch. On inward curves, clip the seam allowance almost to the marked seamline to make turning the edge easier.

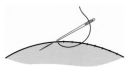

Appliqué stitch

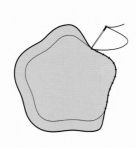

If the background fabric shows through the appliqué, carefully cut away the background fabric to within ¼" of the stitching after appliquéing the shape in place. Another option is to use two layers of appliqué fabric to prevent show-through.

Bias Strips

Bias strips are cut at a 45° angle to the straight grain of the fabric. They are stretchy and therefore ideal for creating curved appliqué stems.

Make the first cut by aligning a 45° guideline on your acrylic ruler with the cut edge or selvage of the fabric. Use this new bias edge to cut strips the required width.

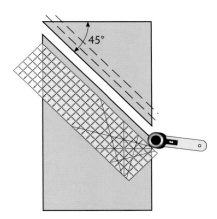

Prepare bias strips for appliqué by folding them in half lengthwise, wrong sides together. Stitch ¼" from the raw edges. Trim the seam allowances to ⅛". Center the seam allowance on the wrong side and press. A bias press bar is helpful for this.

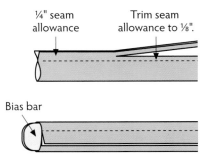

¼" seam allowance

Trim seam allowance to ⅛".

Bias bar

Curved Piecing

Cut pieces using a small-bladed rotary cutter or trace templates and use scissors to maneuver the curves. Make short clips into the concave seam allowance to help with pinning and sewing.

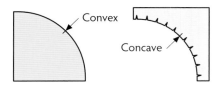

With right sides together, pin the convex piece to the inside curve (concave) of the second piece at the middle, the ends, and a few places in between. Sew with the *concave* piece on top, stopping frequently with the needle down to adjust the fabric so it lies flat under the needle and presser foot. After stitching, press the seam allowances toward the convex piece.

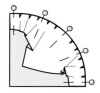

English Paper Piecing

With this method, the fabric pieces are basted around a stiff piece of paper, and then the edges of the prepared pieces are whipstitched together.

Trace and cut a piece of stiff paper for each piece in the design. Place the paper template on the wrong side of the chosen fabric and pin it in place. Cut around the shape, adding a generous ¼" seam allowance all around.

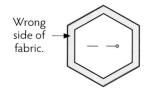

Fold the seam allowance over the edge of the paper template and hold in place. With needle and thread, baste the seam allowance through all thicknesses with long stitches. When you reach the end of the first side, fold over the next seam allowance and continue stitching. Continue in this manner, making sharp folds at each corner, until all the seam allowances are basted in place. For some shapes, the folding will create tails; leave the tails hanging out as shown. Backstitch at the end to secure the stitches. Repeat for each piece needed.

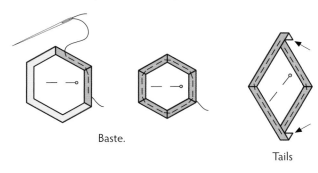

Baste.   Tails

To assemble the block, place the pieces right sides together. With a single strand of thread, whipstitch them together from corner to corner, catching only the folded edges. Repeat to join all pieces. When all edges have been joined, clip the basting threads and remove them from each piece as instructed with each block. Carefully pull out the paper templates. You can reuse the templates.

Whipstitch.

Foundation Piecing

Make paper copies of each foundation as required for the chosen block. Sew pieces to the foundation in numerical order. Center the first fabric under space #1, with the wrong side of the fabric against the unprinted side of the paper. The piece should extend beyond the seam allowances on all sides. Pin in place from the paper side.

Turn the piece with the fabric side up. Using a piece of fabric sufficient to cover space #2 and its seam allowances, position piece #2 right sides together on piece #1 as shown, aligning the edges to be sewn. The edge of the piece should extend at least ¼" into the space #2 area. Pin in place.

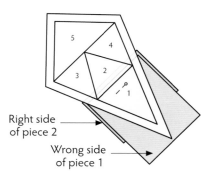

Right side of piece 2

Wrong side of piece 1

Set your sewing machine for a very short stitch length (18–20 stitches per inch or 1.5 mm). Turn the unit paper side up. Stitch through the paper and the fabric layers along the printed seamline, beginning and ending ¼" beyond the ends of the line.

Turn the unit to the fabric side. Trim the seam allowances to approximately ¼". Press so that space #2 is covered.

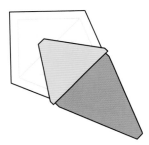

Repeat this process to complete the blocks or sections, allowing at least ¼" of fabric to extend beyond the edge of the paper. Use a rotary cutter and ruler to trim ¼" outside the seamline of the foundation, creating the seam allowance. The printed foundation patterns include the outer seam allowances, so you'll be trimming on the outer lines. Once all the seams around a foundation have been sewn, carefully remove the paper foundation.

Triangle Squares

With right sides together and the lighter fabric on top, layer one square of each color as instructed for the block you're making. On the lighter square, draw a diagonal line from corner to corner. You may draw the diagonal line before or after layering the squares. Stitch ¼" from both sides of the line. Cut apart on the marked line.

With the darker fabric on top, open out the top piece and press. Trim the dog-ear points at the corners. Each pair of squares will yield two identical half-square-triangle units.

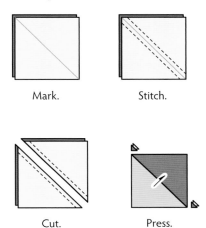

Mark.   Stitch.

Cut.   Press.

Fast Flying Geese

Align two small squares on opposite corners of a larger square, right sides together. Draw a diagonal line through both squares as shown, and then stitch ¼" from both sides of the line. Cut apart on the marked line.

With the small triangles on top, open out the triangles and press.

On the remaining corner of each of these units, align a small square. Draw a line from corner to corner and sew ¼" from both sides of the line. Cut on the marked lines, open the small triangles, and press. Each set of one large square and four small triangles makes four identical flying-geese units.

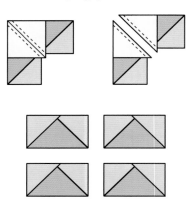

Stitch and Flip

Align a square on a corner of a larger square, a rectangle, or a pieced unit as directed in the block instructions. Mark a diagonal line on the square from corner to corner. You may have already drawn this line; just make sure you place it slanting in the correct direction. Sew on the marked line. Trim the seam allowances to ¼" as shown. Flip the resulting triangle open and press.

Yo-Yos

Using the circle diameter called for in the block pattern (approximately twice the finished yo-yo size, plus ½"), make a template. On the wrong side of the chosen fabric, use the template to trace a circle. Cut out the circle on the marked line.

Turn under a scant ¼" to the wrong side of the fabric. Sew a basting stitch around the circle, leaving a knot and thread tail at the beginning of the circle.

Pull on the threads to gather the fabric, making sure the right side of the fabric is on the outside of the yo-yo. Take a few stitches to secure the gathering stitches and tie off. Clip the threads close to the knot. Flatten the yo-yo with the gathered edge in the center.

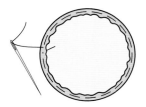

Embroidery Basics

Hand embroidery requires very little in the way of special tools. It's time-honored hand sewing that anyone can do. Using a hoop to stitch is optional. You'll need a small one, about 4" in diameter, for the blocks in this book. Try stitching without one; if you're happy with the results, don't worry about a hoop.

BASIC EMBROIDERY SUPPLIES

Here's what you'll need for the embroidered blocks:

- Large-eye embroidery needle
- Embroidery floss, heavy thread, or pearl cotton
- Pencil or water-soluble fabric marker
- Water-soluble embroidery stabilizer (optional)
- Light box (optional)
- Small hoop (optional)

TRANSFERRING THE DESIGN

The simplest way to transfer the embroidery design is to trace it directly onto the background fabric with a water-soluble marking pen. Some people mark lightly with a very sharp or mechanical pencil or a Pigma pen, later covering these marks with their stitching. To help see the design, use a light box or tape the pattern and fabric to a sunny window. You can also use a water-soluble stabilizer, tracing the design onto the stabilizer first. Adhere the stabilizer to the background fabric, stitch the design through it, and then remove the stabilizer by soaking the piece in water. Look for this product in shops that sell other needlework supplies and follow the manufacturer's instructions.

EMBROIDERY STITCHES

Backstitch

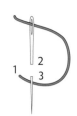 

Blanket stitch

 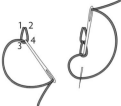

Chain stitch

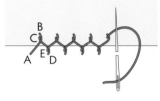

Cretan stitch

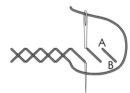

Cross-stitch

Feather stitch

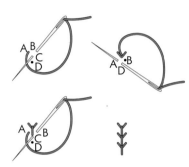

Fly stitch

French knot
(2 winds)

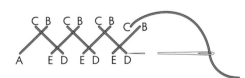

Herringbone stitch

Lazy daisy or
detached chain stitch

Outline stitch
or stem stitch

Running stitch

Satin stitch

60-Block Four Patch and Chain ▪ 65" × 78"

Pieced by Pat Sloan and Roberta Miglin, quilted by Melissa Corry.
For instructions on making this quilt, visit ShopMartingale.com/SS17.

38 Stars ● 84" × 98"
Designed by Pat Sloan and Jane Davidson, pieced by
Kim Niedzwiecki and Pat Sloan, and quilted by Penny Barnes.
For instructions on making this quilt, visit ShopMartingale.com/SS17.

30-Block Faux on Point ▪ 58½" × 70½"

Designed by Pat Sloan, pieced by Melanie Barrett, and quilted by Debby Brown.
For instructions on making this quilt, visit ShopMartingale.com/SS17.

30-Block Red-and-White ▪ 40½" × 47½"

Designed and pieced by Tammy Vonderschmitt; quilted by Maggi Honeyman.
For instructions on making this quilt, visit ShopMartingale.com/SS17.

100-Block Sampler • 80" × 80"
Assembled by Melanie Barrett and quilted by Debby Brown.
For instructions on making this quilt, visit ShopMartingale.com/SS17.

BLOCK INDEX

ABOUT THE AUTHORS

Meet Jane Davidson

I have a love affair with quilting, have always been a bit of a crafty person, and can honestly say I wake up every morning happy in the fact that I love what I do: designing, publishing, long-arm quilting, and teaching. Designing is my favorite part of the quilting experience, and I jump at the opportunity to make an original pattern for a magazine or book. Visit me at QuiltJane.com to see what's new.

Meet Pat Sloan

I'm a quilt designer, author, teacher, radio/podcast show producer and host, and fabric designer. My passion for making quilts, sharing quilts, and talking with quilters about quilts is limitless. I travel to teach and I host several Internet groups of quilters where we share on a daily basis what we make. And I write about quilting on my website. To find me, go to PatSloan.com, sign up for my newsletter, and let's chat soon!